A B U S E D

CONQUERED...

ALIVE!!!

BY,
MARY PROCTOR REED

Abused, Conquered, Alive!!!

Mary Proctor Reed

iUniverse, Inc.
Bloomington

Abused, Conquered, Alive!!!

iUniverse books may be ordered through booksellers or by contacting:

iUniverse
1663 Liberty Drive
Bloomington, IN 47403
www.iuniverse.com
1-800-Authors (1-800-288-4677)

Because of the dynamic nature of the Internet, any web addresses or links contained in this book may have changed since publication and may no longer be valid. The views expressed in this work are solely those of the author and do not necessarily reflect the views of the publisher, and the publisher hereby disclaims any responsibility for them.

Any people depicted in stock imagery provided by Thinkstock are models, and such images are being used for illustrative purposes only.

Certain stock imagery © Thinkstock.

ISBN: 978-1-4759-5269-8 (sc)
ISBN: 978-1-4759-5268-1 (e)
ISBN: 978-1-4759-5270-4 (dj)

Library of Congress Control Number: 2012918036

Printed in the United States of America

iUniverse rev. date: 10/4/2012

You are Abused and You are Conquered, but My book will make You Alive!

This book will make you feel good and be happy about yourself. Hurtful things have happened to you, and you do not deserve to be punished by them. People like to be mean to you and abuse you, and that is not your fault. By the time you get through reading this book, "Abused, Conquered, Alive", you will be stronger than you could have ever imagined because all of those hurtful things will be conquered.

The reason I am writing "Abused, Conquered, Alive", is to help healing come to everybody that has painful memories from anything that has happened to them and their family, because all of us have gone through very bad things, and it is certainly a miracle that any of us survived them. In order to go on with our lives, we must conquer the enemies of the nature that is within all of us to give in to those memories and give up. We need to fight to stay alive and live each day that we can, and we have to conquer the enemy that is with each and every one of us all the time.

In this book, "Abused, Conquered, Alive" you will find out what really happened. This is a true account of the events that happened, to the best of my knowledge. All the names of the people in this book are the actual people, and, these are the real places where things happened.

Abused, Conquered, Alive!

This book is about how hurtful memories of abuse can conquer you of everything good that you want to do with your life, and my hurtful memories over-whelmed me, until, I was dying.

You, too, and everybody else, can remember how much pain you experienced, as abuse from people terrorizes your memories that you cannot erase, because those hurtful things in your mind do not go away. And when it is suggested to you that you need to get over it, and forget all about the past, the pain from the abuse causes you to get angry, because you did not deserve to be hurt and abused.

People think that you can just get over it, and act like you were never abused! People do not know how badly you are hurt all over again by them, when they deny that you were ever abused, and they say that it was your own fault!

How to get past the abuse that has conquered you is harder than anybody can ever imagine.

That is why I am writing this book, Abused, Conquered, Alive, because I have been abused, and you have been abused, and you are probably still being abused, and I am so sorry. And, the abuse was so bad that it conquered me, and I truly prayed to God to please just take me out of this cruel, old, ugly world because I wanted to die.

CONTENTS

PREFACE

◇◇◇◇◇◇◇◇◇◇◇◇◇◇◇◇◇◇◇◇◇◇◇◇◇◇◇◇◇◇◇◇◇◇◇◇

I was starving because I wanted to get back down to the size I was before my baby was born. However, it took time, and it was hard to keep from eating, because I was so hungry, but I still fixed all of the meals and sat at the table, and I took tiny portions of food on my plate, although, I did not eat enough to keep from being very hungry.

I cried, "I can't help it that my stomach is still fat, and I still look like I'm pregnant, and Michael, you need to look at yourself, because you have a mole on your back that is getting bigger, and you need to have it taken off by a doctor".

I had no idea that the mole on my husband's back was cancerous, and he did not know it was a cancer either, and, as a kind favor to me, Michael agreed to have our family physician take it off. He played a lot of softball in the community and coached softball for our church, and that caused him to be in the sun, so a couple of days later, Michael had an appointment, and he had the mole removed from his back.

1—DON'T DIE

"**D**addy, don't die!"

"Daddy, please, don't die!"

Rachelle cried in terror, as she sat on her daddy's bed next to his pillow frantically watching her big sister, Mary Michelle, help as I gave cardio pulmonary resuscitation to their daddy, Michael, the love of my life.

For the last few years Michael was being eaten up with melanoma cancer. It started out as a little dark brown mole in the middle of his back. Then there was a place that was as big as my hand, if my fingers were spread out that was in the middle of my husband's back, which was where skin and tissue had been removed to save his life.

Skin was taken from a place on one of his thighs, and grafted onto his back to cover up the place where the skin and tissue was gone. The doctor talked to me that said if Michael had not gotten the surgery when he did, within six weeks he might have died.

Throughout the next couple of years, Michael had melanoma skin cancer taken off several areas of his body. Then the melanoma cancer showed up inside of his organs. When he went to the toilet, both urinating and pooping it was red with blood.

After Michael was in the intensive care area of the hospital for a few days, he got to come home. Then he went through a series of chemotherapy treatments that caused him to get weak and very sick to his stomach. He was nauseated and he threw up, so often, that he got to where he would cry real easy. And he was in constant unbearable pain.

Friends came to our home and prayed for him, but he kept on getting sicker. At the same time he was depressed, and he lost his appetite, so he started losing weight.

Then my husband was signed up with hospice, because the doctor said that Michael might only have a few days to live, or a few weeks to live. Although, I never gave up on my husband, and I felt like he would be well and strong again, and he would live, for a long time.

But my husband died!

The young hospice nurse told everybody that was at our home on Lake Ridge Road in Danville, Illinois, to go home, because it was after midnight, and Michael needed to be able to sleep. Ina, the hospice nurse that was in charge of his care would come over, and see my husband in the morning.

And this young hospice nurse would not let anybody listen to me that my husband was too sick to be at home. She said that I was just a nursing student without any experience, and she was an experienced registered nurse with hospice.

She thought that Michael was going to be all right, and that he would still be here in the morning. And she even went to the extent of saying that she promised Michael would still be here in the morning. Then the young hospice nurse made a sign over her heart in the form of a cross, that she was sure that everybody could go on home, and get a good night sleep, because Michael would still be alive in the morning.

He was having trouble breathing, but the hospice nurse got him to take morphine that was prescribed for pain. So she said that he would start breathing better and relax, and then after he got a good night sleep, he would be all right in the morning.

After everybody left our home from seeing Michael, my little daughter, Rachelle, went to bed, and she was so exhausted from all of the company staying so late that she went right to sleep. And we were encouraged that the hospice nurse was so confident that Michael would be all right, after he got to sleep that night.

I stayed in our bedroom and got ready for bed. And I was still very worried about my husband, so I kept my eyes on him, as I prepared myself to go to bed. And of course, I was going to sleep in our bed with my husband, as usual.

Michael was still breathing, and I thought he was going to sleep, so I thought it would be a good time for me to use the restroom that was close to our bedroom, where he was lying on our bed.

I was in the restroom, for maybe ten minutes, and I was brushing my teeth, as I walked back into our bedroom to check on my husband. And I was very much surprised to see Michael looking at me, because he had his eyes closed the entire time that his family and the pastor, and the hospice nurse were at our home.

So I was excited to see that my husband was looking at me, because he had a big smile on his face. And he put his hand up toward me, and motioned for me to come to him.

I quickly put my toothbrush down that I was brushing my teeth with when I was checking on Michael, and hurried over to him. And I thought he wanted me to make love with him, because he was smiling the way he did when we would decide to make love.

So I ran to our bed, and jumped up on our bed, and I was looking at him all of that time. But then his hand fell down on the bed, and I realized that he was not breathing, anymore.

And I looked into Michael's eyes and saw that he had no sparkle in them, and they looked like marbles that had lost their polish.

Then I very quickly rushed towards my husband, and put my face close to his face to see if he was, maybe, breathing real shallow like. But he wasn't that I could tell, so I panicked!

I cried out loud into my husband's face, "Mike!"

And I was right beside my husband, with my face and my lips close to his, hoping he would acknowledge me.

And, I cried out again to my husband because I wanted him to somehow show me some kind of expression, or any kind of life!

I loved and still do love my husband, and he needed to respond to me! But Michael did not breathe, or move, or anything!

So, I quickly placed one of my hands on my husband's forehead and pushed his head back, as I was lifting his chin up with my other hand the way I was taught how to give somebody breaths who was not breathing.

And I quickly placed my mouth on Michael's mouth, and I forced out a long slow breath as best I could. Then I forced out another long slow breath into my husband's mouth.

At the same time I was stifling panicky cries, because I was scared to death that my husband was not breathing, or maybe he was, and I could not hear or see him breathe!

Then I put my fingers on my husband's neck on his carotid artery to check his pulse, to see if he was alive.

Michael could not be dead!

But I could not be so panicky that I lost it, because my husband needed for me to save him!

So, I very quickly positioned my husband's head, so that I was tilting his head backwards with one of my hands, and lifting his chin up with my other hand, enough to keep his mouth open. I gave him two, long, slow, breaths, and I tried to find a pulse on my husband's carotid artery on his neck. I could not find a pulse, so I gave my husband fifteen compressions, as I counted out loud.

Then I very quickly gave my husband two, slow, long, breaths, and I yelled and screamed in my anguish, as loud as I could. So my daughter, Mary Michelle, heard me and came running to me.

I yelled, "Mary Michelle, get up here, your dad's dying!"

Mary Michelle was screaming and crying and waking up her little sister, Mary Rachelle, to come into the bedroom where Daddy was.

And I tried to find a pulse on my husband's carotid artery on his neck, but I could not find a pulse. So I did fifteen chest compressions that were very hard to do, because I was trying my very best to push down on his chest, one and a half to two inches, the way I had been taught in CPR, Cardio Pulmonary Recitation classes.

And I told my oldest daughter, Mary Michelle, to help me give her daddy CPR.

I counted our loud, "One, and two, and three, and four, and five, and six, and seven, and eight, and nine, and ten, and eleven, and twelve, and thirteen, and fourteen, and fifteen".

I gave my husband two more slow, long breaths, and I could hear Mary Michelle, frantically yelling and crying.

Mary yelled, "Rachelle, wake up, Dad's dying!"

Rachelle was sound asleep, and to be told to wake up like that was more than any little girl should, ever, have to go through, in her entire life!

But bless her heart, Mary Michelle was, certainly scared to death, and she needed to help her mommy, so she did not have time to be of comfort to her little sister, or anybody else.

Rachelle just turned eleven-years-old on April 25, and it was May 6, 1993, now, and it was probably around 12:40 am, by now. And she was awakened with a scream from her sister, Mary Michelle that "Dad's dying!"

My little daughter, Rachelle, jumped out of her canopy bed and ran into our bedroom where I was doing CPR on her daddy. She jumped up on our bed, and quickly maintained her position at the top of her daddy's head, because that was where she had been sitting for so long, when Michael's family, Pastor Rogers, and the hospice nurse had been at our home that night. And she had been sitting there, tenderly washing her daddy's forehead and face, with a cool washcloth.

Mary Michelle was on the other side of her daddy, by about the time I had finished saying, "and twelve". She saw me practice doing CPR on a big doll that she had when she was Rachelle's age. And I continued to keep up with CPR classes for several years, so both of my daughters watched me practice doing CPR on the big doll, then they would laugh because the doll's head would pop off, when I gave it chest compressions.

However, I had never done CPR on a person before, and I was doing the very best that I could, as I told Mary Michelle to do the compressions for me.

And she was screaming and crying, and Rachelle was screaming, "Daddy! Don't die!"

I did not know who called Michael's sister, Jeanie, but she was on the phone, and she was hearing what was going on. We had Michael's parents' phone number, and his sister and brother's phone numbers on a paper next to a blue, princess telephone that was on the nightstand, on my side of the bed. So, of course, Jeanie and Keith let everybody know that had been at our home with Michael that night.

Mary Michelle gave her daddy fifteen compressions, that she knew how to do and was doing perfectly. She was so scared that her daddy was dying, that she pushed every bit of two inches into his chest. And I gave my husband two more slow, long breaths, and I told my oldest, daughter, Mary Michelle, to give her daddy fifteen more compressions, and to count out loud.

We did this cycle over and over, for four cycles, and I gave Michael two more, long, slow breaths, and then I rechecked Michael's carotid artery in his neck, but there still was no pulse!

Mary Michelle cried very loudly, as she counted out loud again, and gave her daddy compressions on the lower half of her daddy's sternum, the way she saw me doing it, before she did the compressions for me.

I did all of the breaths into her daddy's mouth, and I held his head tilted backwards, and his chin lifted the way I was taught to do, and we did this for four more cycles. Mary Michelle would give fifteen compressions to my two, long, slow breaths, and then I rechecked Michael's carotid artery in his neck, and there was still no pulse!

Mary Michelle was still screaming and crying out loud, "Mommy, stop, you can't help Dad anymore, it's too late, please, stop, Mommy!"

And, I commanded Mary Michelle, "Keep on giving him compressions and count out loud! I will give him all the breaths; you will not have to give him any breaths!"

I did not want my daughter to have to put her mouth over her daddy's mouth, because it was very slimy. And it smelled like rotten deer meat that I cooked one time that we threw out, because it smelled like poop.

So, Mary Michelle gave her daddy compressions, and she cried out loud, "One, and two, and three, and four, and five, and six, and seven, and eight, and nine, and ten, and eleven, and twelve, and thirteen, and fourteen, and fifteen!"

Then I gave my husband two more, long, slow, deep breaths the way I was taught when I took CPR classes, and I kept his head tilted backwards, and his chin lifted as I gave the breaths.

Then Pastor Rogers and somebody else were suddenly in our bedroom right next to Mary Michelle, who was screaming and crying. And Rachelle was in the room with us, while her sister and I were giving her daddy CPR.

And, I had not said a word to my baby, Rachelle, the entire time that I was trying to save her daddy's life.

Because I was trying my very best to not lose it, and I had to save my husband's life!

I could not allow myself to cry, because I had to do exactly what I needed to do, to try my best to save Michael's life!

Pastor Rogers was next to Mary Michelle, and she was crying and shaking, so badly, that it was a miracle in itself, that my daughter did not have a nervous breakdown, right then and there!

And, it was a miracle that Rachelle my little, baby girl that was verily eleven-years-old did not have a heart attack and die! When her daddy was getting all that CPR done on him for several minutes!

If I had ever thought in a million years that my husband, Michael Proctor the first, was going to die that night, I would have, at the very least, told not only Pastor Rogers to stay. Also, I would have told all of my husband's family to stay, and not leave us alone with Michael. And I would have told my husband's sister, and her husband, to help me get Michael to the emergency room.

Also, my brother-in-law, Keith, had asked me when the hospice nurse was at our home, and Michael was so sick, if I wanted him to call our son, Mike. But I did not think Mike needed to come, because this hospice nurse kept on insisting that my husband was just very tired, because he had not been getting very much sleep, for the last few months. However, I was very glad that Keith went on ahead and called my son.

My son, Mike, got an emergency phone call from his Uncle Keith to come right away, if he wanted to see his dad, because Michael was not looking good, at all. And at that time, my son was in training with the state for a job. And my son's friends were very helpful to him, because they had him immediately get into their vehicle, and drove as fast as they could, all the way to our home, and that was very good.

However, if I had even thought for one moment that his daddy was going to die that night, I would have not only had somebody take Michael to the emergency room at the hospital, I would have also had somebody call Mike a lot sooner than he was called.

After Reverend Rogers came into our home, and heard Mary Michelle and Rachelle crying loudly, he came into the bedroom where I was giving Michael mouth–to-mouth long, deep breaths. And I don't know who all was with him, and I never knew how they all got into our home; because I thought the front door was locked.

Anyway, Reverend Rogers said, "Stop, Mary, he's dead!"

And, that was when I looked up, after I gave my husband, Michael, the second long, deep breath, and I saw Reverend Rogers standing next to my daughter, Mary Michelle, who was just, hysterically, crying!

Then I loosened my hands from off the top of my husband's forehead and his chin, and I gently and lovingly repositioned his head, so that it was lying flat on our bed with his face turned straight up towards the ceiling.

And I crawled under the sheet and blanket that was covering my husband's legs and waist, and I lay as close as I could to him, and sobbed, and sobbed.

I could not let my husband, Michael, die! How could I get him to come back alive to me?

I lay very close to my husband and prayed and sobbed, so uncontrollably, that I just wanted to die right then and there, because I did not want to live without my husband!

Consequently, Pastor Rogers said, "Mary, you need help, who can I call to come and help you?", and as I sobbed, I cried in a broken voice that he could not understand.

However, Mary Michelle said, "I think she said Kim", and they wondered who Kim was.

And as I was still sobbing, and lying close to my husband, I said, "I want my teacher, Kim".

Then Mary Michelle said, "She has a teacher named Kim, I think that's who she wants".

So they called my teacher, Kim, and she immediately came over, even though, by then, it was probably one o'clock in the morning, and she had exams for students to take the next day.

I never knew for sure why I wanted my instructor, Kim, except, that Kim was my counselor all through nursing college. And I had faith in her that she would always know what to do in a crisis, and, of course, there was a huge crisis in our lives at that time.

I stayed there lying under the sheet and blanket as close to my husband as I could, because I did not want him to be dead. And I was praying that all of the life that was in my body would go into my husband, Michael Proctor's body, right then and there, and he would be all right, and, he would be well.

Somehow, I did not process the realization that my husband was actually dead, and I could not handle the thought of him being dead.

Then I realized that our son, Mike, was standing next to the bed, and he had a look of surprise, anguish, and fear all at one time in his eyes, and he did not say anything, at all.

I was surprised to see our son, and I was very glad that he was here with his daddy and me. And, somehow, at that exact moment, I felt secure, and I knew that everything was going to be all right.

Our son, Mike, had to grow up real fast, and become a man when his dad was diagnosed with melanoma skin cancer eleven years earlier.

Mike had to help me one time when his dad needed to go to the emergency room at the hospital, so even with his dad's protests, Mike helped me dress his dad, and we took him to the emergency room.

If we had not done that, their daddy would have, no doubt, died more than six months earlier, right in that bed where he died that night.

Michael never wanted to be in a hospital, or any kind of place, when the time would come that he would die. He was afraid of dying alone, and he did not want to die, at all.

Michael never wanted to die, and leave our children and me without a daddy, because we would be all alone and homeless without him, and something bad would happen to us. My husband had taught me to obey him, because he was the head of our house, and he had convinced me that I could not live without him.

I still would not believe that Michael, the love of my life, was dead, and I did not accept that he was, truly, dead, for a couple of years, after he died.

Michael Dean Proctor, my lover and husband, died from Metastasis Malignant Melanoma Cancer and Plural Spiral Supra-Ventricular Tachycardia Heart Failure.

Kim was helpful to us the night that my husband died, and she came into the bedroom where I was lying very close to my husband. She helped me get up and go into our living room, where I sat with my children and my mother, Flossie, who had been called to come and help us.

I had truly lost it, for a while there, because I could not believe my husband died. And it was an agonizing thing to see people taking my husband, my children's daddy, out of our home on a Gurney, and I certainly did not want Michael to be dead.

And, as I sat next to my beautiful mom and children, with all of our family in our home, I had a driving urge to rush to my husband and scream and cry out to him that he had no right to die and leave us alone. He needed to come back to us because he was our boss, and the father of our children, and we loved him.

I was so, totally, lonely, because I felt completely dependent on Michael to always take care of us. Michael always told me that without him I would be homeless. And nobody would ever want me because I was not smart enough to think for myself, and I kept my nose out of his business like he always told me to, so I needed him, and I loved him, and I could not live without him.

2—THE BATTLE WITH MELANOMA SKIN CANCER

Mary & Michael Proctor Wedding

Picture copyright William O. Fuller Palos Hills, Illinois: Model Release not obtained for subjects of photographs

President Richard M. Nixon was in office when Michael and I got married, July 3, 1970. The weather was hot and humid in Danville, Illinois, and there was no air-conditioning in the Assembly of God Church where the ceremony was held.

I made all of my sisters yellow dresses, and they were all in our wedding. I bought a used wedding dress, and Michael wore a black suit that he had on when he graduated from Central Bible College a couple of days before we got married.

A month after Michael and I got married, we moved two states away from our families. Michael and I moved from Illinois to Kansas, where we lived in the church parsonage that belonged to the Assembly of God Church that Michael became the pastor of.

And we were very close to our families that we left in Illinois, so we missed them, and they missed us a real lot. However, God was in control of our lives, and He had work for us to do for Him.

For the entire four years that Michael was the minister of the Phillipsburg church, he preached on The Love of God and Promises of God, and The Wonderful Plan of God's Salvation.

Before then I thought God was so scary that He would abandon anybody, immediately, if they committed any sin no matter how little. And even a thought of anger against anybody was a reason for God to abandon anybody.

Yes, in the Old Testament it has many places about how God does not tolerate any sin. And in the New Testament it says that nobody is God's child, unless they have believed in God.

God sent His only Begotten Son, the Lord Jesus Christ, into the world to take away everybody's sins. And you must believe in God, and that His Son, Jesus Christ, was crucified and died on the cross for your sins. And you must confess your sins to The Lord Jesus Christ, and ask The Lord Jesus Christ to take all of your sins away, and come into your heart and life.

If you do not do what God tells you to do, in order to get to go to Heaven when you die, you will not be saved from Hell Fire and Brimstone that will burn you, forever and ever.

In other words, if you are not going to Heaven when you die, you are going to die and go to Hell and burn with Satan.

I knew it was impossible for anybody to be perfect.

I certainly was not perfect. And I did not know anybody, except The Lord Jesus Christ that was perfect.

I prayed and cried my heart and soul out to God to help me. And I had accepted The Lord Jesus Christ as my Personal Savior many times in my life. And I felt the closeness of The Holy Spirit, so much, that I could see Christ in my soul.

I was taught, throughout my life in The Assemblies of God churches that I grew up in. And when I went to the churches where my husband, Michael, was the minister, that it is easy to slip away from God. And one sin will keep a person out of Heaven. And I was always afraid I would go to Hell.

What if I sinned and did not know it? And what if I died before I got to confess any sin to God and ask for His forgiveness?

I read "The Holy Bible" many times, and searched the scriptures for help. And I wanted to know about God and what He is like.

The biggest thing preached over and over was that God is Love.

In "The Holy Bible", in John 4:8, it says, "God is Love".

Just think about it.

God loved the people in this earth, so much, that He gave His only Begotten Son to die in our place. So our sins could be taken away. So we can have eternal life.

And if, we believe in The Lord Jesus Christ, and ask Him to take our sins away and come into our life, He does right then and there.

Just think about it, in Philippians 4:19, God tells us that He shall supply all your needs according to His riches in Glory. And that is the Love of God taking care of His creation.

God is our refuge and strength. And you need to run to Him when you have troubles, because God is your refuge.

Run to God! And He shall supply all of your needs. Because God is our refuge, it says so in "The Holy Bible", in Psalms 46:1.

Michael preached many times about Heaven.

In John 14:1 through 6, it says in "The Holy Bible",

> Let not your heart be troubled;
> You believe in God,
> Believe also in me.
> In My Father's house are many mansions
> If it were not so,
> I would have told you.
> I go to prepare a place for you.
> And if I go and prepare a place for you,
> I will come again and receive you to myself;
> That where I am,
> There you may be also.
> And where I go you know,
> And the way you know.

> Thomas said to Him,
> Lord, we do not know where You, *Jesus* are going,
> And how can we know the way?
> Jesus said to him, "I am the way,
> The truth and the life,
> No one comes to the Father except through Me, Jesus".

Michael would say, "It is in John 14 verse 6 that Jesus says, I am the way, the truth, and the life. No one comes to the Father except through me."

That would be his entire topic for his message on going directly to The Lord Jesus Christ when anybody prays to God. And he would say that it was a sin to ask any priest to take away your sins, because only Jesus Christ our Lord and Savior can take away sins.

Michael would preach. "Do not bow down or give allegiance to any statue."

The only way anybody can get to God is by doing what Jesus teaches us in John 14 verse 6. And that is exactly what it says when Jesus says, "No one comes to the Father except through Me"; Jesus is the only way to the Father.

Michael sang many songs to the audiences at churches where he preached. All of the songs had messages in them, and one song that Michael sang was written by LA Verne Tripp, "I've Been Born Again".

I don't want fine mansions here in this world of sin and shame,
All I want to know is that I've been born again;
I don't want wealth or fame,
I don't care who knows my name,
All I want to know is that I've been born again.

I think one of the songs Michael sang that I liked the best was "Jesus Will Outshine Them All," written by Gordon Jensen.

Mansions will glisten on the hills of Glory,
Happy reunions on streets of gold,
Angels choirs singing glad praises forever,
But Jesus will outshine them all!

Oh, what glory awaits me in Heaven's Bright City?
When I get there such sights I'll behold,
A million scenes of rare beauty will demand that I view them,
Still Jesus will outshine them all!

Remember that in John 14: 2, in "The Holy Bible" it says, "In My Father's house are many mansions, I go and prepare a place for you".

After ministering in Phillipsburg for a few years, Michael accepted the pastorate in Eudora. And he continued to preach on God's Salvation Plan.

At the same time, Michael played a lot of softball in the community and coached softball for our church. And that caused him to be in the sun a lot.

Michael was golden brown most of the time, and looking good was important to him. But that also meant that he expected his wife to look good. And he thought that in order for me to look good, I had to be skinny.

Michael was angry at me, and making fun of me because he said I was fat. And he told me that I had to lose weight, because he was not going to have a fat wife.

So I cried and buried my face in my hands, as I said, "You need to look at yourself, because you have a mole on your back that is getting bigger, and you need to have it taken off by a doctor".

I had no idea that the mole on my husband's back was cancerous. And, of course, he did not know it was a cancer either.

But, as a kind favor to me, Michael agreed to have our family physician take it off. So a couple of days later, Michael had an appointment, and he had the mole removed from his back.

The biopsy showed that Michael had melanoma skin cancer.

He was entered into a Kansas City Medical Center and surgery was done. And all of the lymph nodes around any areas that might have the melanoma cancer were removed.

That was a real prayer need.

Michael was a chosen man of God.

Michael preached The Word of God. And we believed in miracles.

So I thanked God for using me to be a vessel of His, to tell my husband about the mole on his back, or he would not have gone to the doctor and had it removed.

Now, here was Michael in the hospital, and we were worried about him, because he had melanoma skin cancer. And we hoped and prayed that the physician got all of the cancer out, and that it would not come back.

However, over the next three years, Michael had places come up on his skin that all had to be cut off, because they were all melanoma skin cancer.

After that, Michael never felt very good. And for the first three years he had continual surgeries, which were all melanoma cancer cells.

Then for five years the cancer went into remission, but after that Michael started having feelings of doom!

He would say there was something wrong with himself; even though, the five years without cancer seemed to show that he was all right.

The physician said, since Michael did not show signs of having cancer on his skin after five years, he was considered to be over the cancer.

However, Michael started feeling worse and worse. So we went to the physician that took care of Michael's treatment and surgeries.

Again, he had several places that were melanoma skin cancer cut off his body. And Michael got a complete physical, and blood work was done.

The physician saw a place that did not look right, which was on his liver. And it turned out that it was, also cancer. Then Michael had surgery done on his liver to remove all of the cancer, which was also melanoma cancer.

Michael was given only a few short weeks to live, because the cancer kept spreading throughout other organs in his body.

I was almost conquered when I went to see my husband in the hospital. However, I had been reading in God's "Holy Bible", that we needed to forgive and love one another.

So I forgave anybody who ever hurt me in my lifetime. And I would try real hard to never do anything to cause pain to people. But I knew that sometimes I would hurt people because nobody is perfect.

That was why my husband, Michael, was afraid to die. He was licensed and ordained with the Kansas district in the early 1970's, and he had been the preacher at two churches, and he was afraid of God.

He was afraid God would get him for treating anybody mean. But I told my husband, over and over, that God would not hurt him, because God is a loving and merciful God.

From the first time that Michael was diagnosed with melanoma skin cancer, he insisted that this sickness was caused because he was mean, and I always told him that it was, just, what happened to us.

Michael got melanoma cancer and that meant we both had it, because when one partner in a marriage got something, it was something we both had to deal with.

I loved and still do love Michael, and I took real good care of him throughout our marriage, and when he had the cancer.

In fact, I babied my husband to pieces, and he liked all of the attention I always gave him. He liked the love that we shared, and I always liked the attention that Michael gave to me, too.

Before Michael and I were married, he gave me a nickname that he almost always called me, and I love it. Michael called me, "Beautiful", and he said that was exactly what I was. He always told me how much he loved me, and I always told him that I loved him.

The most important way to be beautiful was on the inside. Because beauty from within is far greater than beauty on the outside, and he always said that I was both.

Michael worked as much as he could, and he was a real good provider for our family. And he worked hard fixing up the homes that we lived in.

Michael always took on extra jobs to earn money to help pay for gas, because we picked up people and brought them to church. And we took them to places that they needed to go, like to hospitals or nursing homes, and appointments or stores.

Also, we took people to camp and meetings that Michael worked in. And we sponsored people and children who wanted to go to camp and meetings.

My husband taught people about The Words of God in "The Holy Bible". Broad is the way that leads to destruction, and narrow is the way that leads to life. Few will enter into the Kingdom of God. Many people think that they will go to Heaven, but many of those people will go to Hell, because God is not mocked. And, only the righteous few will enter into Eternal Life.

Michael preached that God let punishments come upon His people in The Old Testament for sinning.

So when Michael was diagnosed with melanoma cancer, he said it was God punishing him for being mean to me.

No, it was not, I told Michael, over and over, because it, just, happened that Michael got cancer! Because he got cancer! And God was not punishing him.

I believed, and still do believe that people get cancer, or something bad happens to them because that is life. And, it is a fact that people get sick.

And Michael got sick with cancer, and I got to take care of my husband. And I liked taking care of him, and I gave him my life.

But I did not give Michael my soul. I gave my soul to Jesus, when I accepted Him as my Personal Savior, after He took my sins away.

But, with all of the prayers for Michael to get well, he still died.

3—PREGNANT

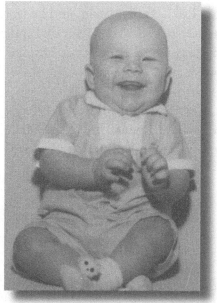

My Baby Mike

After I got pregnant for my first baby, Mike, I prayed day and night for this child of mine. And I saw my baby in dreams and visions. Then the Holy Spirit would come upon me, as I was be praying. And I would see my baby, Mike, and, that was exactly what God gave to me.

Before the doctor would dismiss Baby Mike and me from the hospital, we had to prove that there was a qualified adult who would be in our home to take care of us, before we went home.

It was in early May, of 1971, and President Nixon was still in office, and there were anti-Vietnam war protests, in which thirteen thousand protesters were arrested. And my sister, Linda, and her little son, Robbie, got on a bus.

They traveled on different buses, all the way from Benton, Illinois, to Phillipsburg, Kansas. Then Michael picked them up from the bus station, which was actually at a downtown restaurant. So after being in the hospital for almost two weeks, I got to go home.

Linda worked hard taking care of our new baby, her little three year old son, Robbie, and me. Also, she cooked all of the meals for my husband and us, and, of course, she kept our laundry done and the house clean because a lot of company came to see Baby Mike and me.

After a few days Robbie kept crying, and he would not eat. He had a fever, and he was very sick. So Michael took Linda and Robbie to the doctor, and Robbie was admitted into the hospital. Then Robbie was diagnosed with meningitis, and he was critical, so he was kept in the hospital for several days.

When he was released from the hospital, he could not come back to our home, because we had a new baby. Then Michael took Linda and Robbie home from the hospital all the way back to Benton, Illinois.

Little Mike with his mommy, me

Michael and I were still living in the Phillipsburg Assembly of God Church parsonage three years later, in April of 1974. When 148 tornados covering a dozen states killed 315 people and injured 5500. And gold hit a record of $197.00 an ounce.

About that same time, God gave us another baby, on April 11, 1974. We had a beautiful, baby girl, and she weighed nine pounds, eight ounces. She was so perfect, and her eyes were the prettiest, big, blue eyes that I had ever seen.

In fact, this new baby girl was so beautiful that her daddy got upset to say the least. And Michael again said very unkind things to me, just like he did the first time he came into my hospital room after Little Mike was born, because he did not get enough attention from the doctor who delivered our baby.

Things did not go well with this new baby's birth, either. Because the night before she was born, I was uncomfortable, and I hurt all over.

Then in the morning I told Michael that my stomach hurt, and I did not feel good, and I was real tired. But Michael was tired, too, because I had tossed and turned so much during the night that it kept him from getting a good night's sleep.

Well, Michael said he needed to get his sleep, so, if I wanted to go to the doctor, I could just walk. And I needed to take our little son, Mike, because my husband, Michael, was not going to be bothered with him. Because my husband was tired, and he needed to get some sleep.

I got Mike ready, but I was doubling over in pain, as I started out the door. And the pains were getting worse and worse, about every fifteen minutes. And I cried to Michael, but he told me to let him get some sleep, because I could tell him what the doctor said, when I got home.

Mike liked to go for walks with me, and he could tell that something was wrong with me, so he held tightly onto my hand. And I did not have a stroller to put my little son in, so I could hold onto something when I would double over in pain, as we walked. Because the only stroller we used, was one that was loaned to us for a few months when our son was a baby. Then, of course, I did not have it any longer, because our son was almost three years old, and my friend needed it back for her baby.

It was a long two blocks from our home to my friend's house, who I could count on to take care of Mike, while I went on to the doctor's office. Then after I left Mike at her house, I walked slowly to the doctor's office that was another five or six long blocks. And I stopped and doubled up in pain, every fifteen minutes all the way there.

When I was in the doctor's office I got an examination, and I was told that my baby would be born that morning, so I needed to go to the hospital. Although, I had time to go home, and get my clothes and things that I wanted with me in the hospital.

But the doctor and nurse did not know that I walked over eight blocks to their office. And I would be walking back home by myself.

I was in a lot of pain, and I was doubling over, as I left the doctor's office and started walking back home. The contractions were still fifteen minutes apart, but they were getting harder with each one of them. To make matters worse, I had not eaten any breakfast and I was hungry, and I felt hot and sweaty. Although, it was a nice, cool, spring morning.

By the time I got to my friend's house to pick up Mike, I was having a very difficult time to say the least. But I always kept any problems away from people that my husband and I had. So I did not let my friend take me home when she wanted to, because I only had a couple of blocks left to go.

My little son, Mike, was concerned about me as we walked, because I would stop and lean over. He could see that I was holding onto my stomach with one hand, as he tightly held onto my other hand. And it was all I could do to keep from laying down on the ground. Although, we slowly walked home, and Mike kept telling me that he loved me, all the way home.

When we got home Michael was sound asleep in bed, and he woke up and wanted to know what the doctor said.

I told my husband that the doctor said I needed to go to the hospital, because I was in labor, and my contractions were fifteen minutes apart. So, my husband was happy, and he said that he was going to be part of this delivery.

Then Michael prepared me for the delivery of our baby, and I was in awful pain, as I went to the toilet.

I cried out in pain, "Oh, that's our baby's head! Michael, I need to go to the hospital right now! Please, take me to the hospital Michael, our baby is going to drop inside the toilet! I can't stand it, Michael, please take me to the hospital!"

Well, Michael was happy and he helped me up off the toilet. I tried to walk with him down the hallway and down all of the twelve steps, but it was extremely hard because I felt like I was going to pass out from all of my exhaustion and the excruciating pain. But, somehow, with my husband's help, I got into the back seat of our car and lay down.

It seemed like an eternity, while I waited for my husband to get Little Mike into the front seat of our car. Little Mike held onto his blue blanket, and turned around in the seat, so he could watch me. Then Little Mike asked me if I was tired, and he asked me if I was okay.

I just wanted to hold my precious, cute, little boy so badly, and I was having an extremely hard time not to cry. I did not, ever, want my Little Mike to have to worry about me, or anything else.

My husband dropped our little boy off at my friend's house that was about two blocks away from our home, where we lived in the church parsonage. And then my husband kept on laughing and saying that his wife did not fix him any breakfast, so he guessed that meant he would not get to eat, unless he got his own food. So Michael stopped at a fast food restaurant, and ordered himself some hamburgers, fries and pop.

During that time I was praying in my mind that God would, please, not let my baby come before Michael got me to the hospital. And by the time we got to the hospital that was only about two miles from our home, I was losing consciousness. But I could tell that we stopped, and my husband got out of the car. Then the back door was opened where I was lying on the seat, and I was quickly put on a cot.

I was hurried into the delivery room, and when I woke up our doctor came into the room to check on me, and he told me that I had a baby girl. He also told me that if I had not gotten to the hospital when I did, my baby and I would have both died, because I was torn, and he had to finish making an opening to get the baby out.

So I had 125 stitches again, just like I had from the birth of my last baby, Little Mike. And I had lost consciousness, right after I was brought to the hospital. So he was concerned about my health, but my baby girl was perfect, and she was beautiful.

My desire in life was to be the good, righteous, Godly wife and mother that God made me for. So, of course, I promised Michael that

I would always obey him. And I would never tell anybody details about how he controlled me, or talk about our problems to people. It was alright for me to mention them, and say a little something about how Michael got me to obey him, so people would know that nobody was perfect.

Well, when the nurse brought my new baby girl into my room for me to hold, I cried because I was so happy.

No wonder, this beautiful, baby girl was so beautiful. I prayed for her, the entire time that I carried her.

Baby Mary Michelle

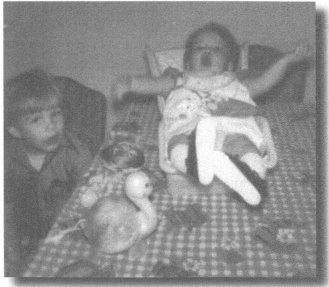

Little Mike & Baby Mary Michelle

How could I go wrong, covering my babies that I was pregnant for, in the Holy Words of The Holy God? And both of my babies, Mike and Mary Michelle, looked like angels to me when they were born.

I could just see bright clouds of light all around Little Mike and Michelle, as I held them in my arms. And I wept great tears of joy unto my Lord in thanksgiving, when I was alone and held my babies.

Because I knew they were both gifts that God was letting me borrow to bring happiness to me. And I would give account to God for how I taught them. Yes, Mike and Mary Michelle were my little angels that God let me borrow, and these babies are truly angels that I love.

I had my baby's name all picked out because God was going to give me a baby girl, and her name was going to be after me, and a cute little girl, Michelle, who was in a children's church class that I taught. So her daddy and I named her after me, because he wanted a baby just like me, and that looked like me, because he was so in love with me, and I was so in love with my husband, Michael.

The hospital staff wanted us to pay our bills, but we did not have the money. So Michael took our baby and me out of the Phillipsburg, Kansas, hospital against the protests of the faculty, and that caused a policeman to try to arrest Michael.

However, the policeman had to let him go, because we signed a paper that the hospital was not responsible for any further procedures that needed to be done for my newborn baby or me. The hospital staff did not want us there if we could not pay the bills, so they let Michael take us home, with the promise that there would be somebody waiting for us at home to take care of us.

There actually was nobody at our home in the church parsonage when we got there, because we forgot to call my sister, Linda, and ask her to, please come and help us, and she lived hundreds of miles away, clear in Illinois.

It was very chilly and it was raining, as we left the hospital that night, and I was so weak that I could not walk without Michael's help. So he had me take several strong pain pills.

Our tiny baby did not have a good night for her first home coming.

Michael was upset because our new baby kept crying, and I had so many stitches that I was bleeding quite a bit, and I must have lost consciousness. But, somehow, I could verily see Michael, as I saw his hand land twice on our new baby's bottom. Although, our baby had a thick diaper on, it really upset me, but I could not do something about it because I was losing consciousness. I did not remember anything else, until I woke up, and there was quite a bit of blood in bed with me, and it was morning.

And I quickly got off the bed, and hurried to the yellow basinet that was right next to the bed with my new, little baby in it.

I was scared to death that my baby was dead! But, she started faintly crying about the time I was picking her up.

I cried, as I very carefully picked up my tiny baby. "Oh, Baby Michelle, Mommy's here now, and I will never let anything bad happen to you again! I love you more than anyone in the whole, wide world, and you are my baby".

At that very moment, my little boy, Mike, came into the bedroom and looked up at me, as I was holding my baby and talking to her. Because when I picked up my baby and held her close to me, she stopped crying, and Mike asked, "Mommy, do you still love me, too?"

I motioned for my little boy to come close to me, as I tenderly held my baby. And I said to Mike, "Yes, Mikie, you are my baby, too. I have always loved you, and I will always love you as much as our new little baby. Her name is Mary Michelle, and she is your baby and my baby, is that okay with you, Mikie?"

Mikie stood close to me, as I held Mary Michelle, and he looked at her very intently, for just a moment. And then he said, "That's my baby and your baby, Mommy".

I could see Michael from a window and he was outside mowing the grass. Then I called a friend, and insisted that she would not let my husband know that I called her, because I knew that I had to always do exactly what my husband taught me to, or he would get mad at me.

No matter what it was, I was taught to be in complete submission throughout my entire life, and I was conquered, so I seldom tried to defend myself. Anybody could control me when they were being authoritative, and when people are in a high position everybody thinks that they are perfect, and people would always believe anything that they said.

I asked my friend to please come and take my babies to her house for a few days, because I was not able to take care of them and myself; I was not actually dismissed from the hospital yet, even though my husband brought me home.

Little Pumpkin was the nickname I used to call Mary Michelle, although I don't think I ever told her that I was the first one who started calling her that name.

Little Mike had a plastic pumpkin that was left over from the last Halloween party that he would give to our Baby Michelle to play with. So I would tell Little Mike that the pumpkin was as big as our baby, and we would laugh and laugh.

Michael, Little Mike, & me holding Mary Michelle

Me with Mary Michelle & Little Mike

4—Abort this Baby

◇◇◇◇◇◇◇◇◇◇◇◇◇◇◇◇◇◇◇◇◇◇◇◇◇◇◇◇◇◇◇◇◇◇

After I got pregnant for the third time, it was not long before I got sick, and I was about five months along, but I was having contractions. I was admitted into the hospital, and a sonogram was taken that showed the baby's head was too big. We were told the baby would be born with water on the brain, also, the physician showed us that this baby was definitely going to be a boy. And after doing some tests, one of the doctors advised us to have this baby terminated.

It is very important to feel safe around somebody. People need to be able to talk with somebody who will not talk about private things that they have shared in confidentiality. And that was what I needed when Peggy and Larry Wright adopted me a few years after my dad died.

Michael and I lived two states away from our families, and it was a rare occasion when I got to talk on the phone to one of my sisters. Although, Michael and his parents talked every weekend, and any other time they wanted to for at least an hour. Also, his parents would call him and come to visit us. And every time we got to see them it was nice, and we all got along. But I was just very lonely, to share things with my family.

Peggy and Larry loved our little family of four the first time they saw us, when they came to the Assembly of God Church in Eudora, Kansas, where Michael was the minister. We spent a lot of time together, and Peggy loved me so much that she wanted our family to be her family.

The times that Peggy had been pregnant she had miscarried, so they did not have any living children. Since a stepparent has to legally adopt children that come into a marriage, the children are not considered legally theirs, so I was considered an orphaned child.

After Peggy and Larry adopted me, it was a honeymoon for a while, because we ate together, and went places together. And we had Christmas together that year, because every time I was pregnant the doctors would tell us not to go far from their offices.

Then I had good friends, from the church come over for dinner on New Year's Eve; which was not unusual for me because I had people over for dinner often. And I liked to cook, and everybody that I knew liked to eat.

Then the Sunday after New Years, Peggy and Larry were eating with us in a restaurant, and I felt contractions. My baby was not due to be born for another four or five months, but the contractions did not stop. Then I was admitted into the Lawrence Hospital in Kansas, and I was prepared for delivery. But my baby did not come, and even with medication going into my veins, our baby was not being born.

I was there for several days, and medications were being given to me to help my baby go ahead and be born. Then a doctor would talk to Michael, and tell him that my life was in danger. Because the contractions kept coming for the entire time that I was in the hospital, and the medications made the contractions so strong, that I was in unbearable pain.

Michael was not a crier, and he tried so hard to keep from crying. He was calling his parents and praying church friends from all around, and they were forming prayer chains. And since the phone that Michael used was right next to the hospital bed where I was laying, I could hear what he was saying.

His parents wanted to come and visit us, and help take care of Mike and Mary Michelle. But Michael told them not to come at that time, because Peggy and Larry were taking care of Mike and Mary Michelle. Then other people in the Eudora Assembly of God Church were taking care of them, but our children were worried about what was going on.

The only time I was away from Mike and Mary Michelle very much was when I worked at the bank in Eudora, Kansas. Then they had a bad experience because the bank got robbed, while I was at work. When anybody tried to contact any of the employees that worked there at that time, they were told they could not talk to them, or see them.

Now that I was in the hospital having problems with contractions, Michael did not let anybody come and see me. Because he was afraid I was going to die, and his nerves were getting worse by the hour. Michael tried to be so strong that he would not let anybody see him like that. And he would not let the people that adopted me come in and see me.

A hospital counselor came into the hospital room where I was having hard contractions, and talked with us. Then another doctor came into the room, and counseled with us. Tests had confirmed that the baby was a boy with an enlarged head. Also, the baby would be disfigured and retarded, because I was being given medications for my health to try and stabilize my condition.

However, between the contractions that I was having before I came into the hospital, and the medications that I was getting to cause this baby to go ahead and be born, I might have more difficulties. So, the best thing to do was for us to sign papers allowing the doctors to go ahead and terminate my pregnancy.

That physician said, "The baby will be aborted".

Then the physician explained that all you have to do is to sign these papers, and just one signature will be good enough. Since Mary is in so much pain, and you are the father, Michael, you can sign your name. And we'll get right with the procedure, and you'll get to take Mary home, before you know it.

I yelled, "Do not sign any papers! Michael, if you sign anything, and my baby is terminated, I'll never be able to get over that! Do not take my baby away from me, because I will never give up my baby! And you two doctors, or whoever you are, leave my baby alone, because I will have my baby! I do not care what condition my baby is in, and I do not care if I die! I want my baby, and only God will take my baby away from me!"

I was yelling and crying, so a couple of nurses came into the room and checked me. And the counselor and doctor stood next to the bed and listened to me.

Michael said, "You heard her, she wants the baby, and I won't sign any papers, because I love my wife. And she has the final say in this, so please, God, don't let my beautiful wife die!"

The technicians left the room, and it was not long before the doctor came back in, and dismissed me from the hospital. Because he said the medication that was being used to help the contractions make the baby to be born needed to be discontinued. And we could see if the contractions would stop without the medication. But if they continued, the baby would probably abort on its own, without a doctor's help.

It was a weird thing, because a few months later, that doctor died of heart failure and he was only around fifty years old.

I got to go back home, and Mike and Mary Michelle got to come home from where they were staying with friends, while I was in the hospital.

The contractions did not quit, however, they got more tolerable. And I was taking medicine that was given to me in the hospital, because my thyroid levels were off. And I took it exactly as prescribed by the doctor, also, we kept every doctor appointment, and I took vitamins daily.

When I was pregnant with my babies I would read to them. I read the entire Bible to my babies. Often, I prayed over my little baby that I was still pregnant with. And I promised God, that if He would let me have my baby, I would always give Him the glory for that, and I made promises to God,

> I would always be His child, and He would always be my God!
> I would always raise my children to serve Him, and give Him thanks!
> Daily, I would acknowledge that everything belongs to God!

I had already known about God, and taught children about God. However, I needed to, actually, make promises to God. And He gave us the example of making promises in "The Holy Bible".

Like, in John 3:16 it says,
> "For God so loved the world that He gave His only Begotten Son, that whosoever believes in Him shall not perish but have Everlasting life…" *That is a promise from God!*

John 3:17 says,
> "For God did not send His Son into the world to condemn the World, but that the world through Him might be saved…"

John 3:18 says,
> "He who believes in Him is not condemned; but he who does
> Not believe is condemned already, because he has not believed
> In the name of the only begotten Son of God..."

John 3:35-36 says,
> "The Father loves the Son, and has given all things into His
> hand. He who believes in the Son has everlasting life; and
> he who does not Believe the Son shall not see life, but the
> wrath of God abides on him.

Then in John 4:23-24 people are taught how to worship God.
> "But the hour is coming, and now is, when the true
> worshipers will Worship the Father in spirit and truth; for
> the Father is seeking such To worship Him! God is Spirit,
> and those who worship Him must Worship in spirit and
> truth".

John 14:15 through 21 says,
> "If you love me keep my commandments. And I will pray
> the Father, and He will give you another helper, that He
> may abide with you forever—The Spirit of truth, whom
> the world cannot receive, because it neither sees Him nor
> knows Him; but you know Him, for He dwells with you
> and will be in you.

> I will not leave you orphans; I will come to you. A little
> while longer And the world will see me no more, but you
> will see me.

> Because I live, you will live also. At that day you will know
> that I am in my, Father, and you in me, and I in you. He
> who has my commandments and keeps them, it is he who
> loves me.

And he who loves me will be loved by My Father, and I will love him and manifest myself to him."

In John 14:23 it says,
"If anyone loves me, he will keep my word; and My Father will love him and we will come to him and make our home with him.

John 14:26 says,
"But the Helper, The Holy Spirit whom the Father will send in my name, He will teach you all things, And bring to your remembrance all things that I said to you."

The Holy Spirit was helping me, as the painful contractions continued for several weeks. And I would cry alone, when Mike and Mary Michelle were in school.

Church in Eudora, Kansas, where Michael was the minister

Michael was the minister at the Assembly of God Church in Eudora, for several years, during which most of that time we lived in our church parsonage, until we started buying our first home.

Then I got pregnant, so a lot of friends were praying for me because something was wrong with my baby, although, the sweetest prayers were from my children, Mike and Mary Michelle.

Mike would pray, "God, please heal my mommy and our baby".

Mary Michelle would pray, "Jesus, please heal my mommy, and don't let Mommy's baby die".

They were so dedicated to God, and they prayed often. They never missed Sunday school and church, for they went with their daddy when I was too sick to go, because I was pregnant with my baby that was growing inside of me.

Before then we never missed because Michael was the minister, also, I taught in many of the activities. Anyway, we would never have missed going to God's house when the doors were open, because that was just the way it was with our family. We were all about God and going to church, because God was and always will be our entire life.

Children are so precious to God and to me. A lot of what I believe is written in chapter 16, of my book "Abused, Conquered, Alive", which is what the Royal Ranger, and Missionette programs in the Assemblies of God teach. I whole-heartedly believe in everything they teach. Also, the children learned integrity, and respect for others and themselves.

Then I had a lot of fun teaching the children in my groups how to do crafts, and cooking and sewing. Also, I taught them about the love of God, and how to pray directly to God.

It is all so simple, yet, so majestic! Our Majesty King of Kings and Lord of Lords, Jesus, taught us how to pray in "The Holy Bible"! And He did not tell us to go to his mother, and ask her to pray for us.

Jesus said, to pray this way:

> Our Father which art in Heaven hallowed be thy name
> Thy kingdom come thy will be done in earth,
> As it is in Heaven…
> Give us this day our daily bread,
> And forgive us our debts,
> As we forgive our debtors.

And lead us not into temptation,
But deliver us from evil:
For yours is the kingdom,
And the power,
And the glory,
Forever...
Amen.

I promised God that I would always serve Him, and I would bring up my children to serve Him, and I kept my word.

So no matter if God chose to heal my little baby that I was going to have or not, I would still trust in Him, because God is my God. There is only one God, yet, there is the trinity, God the Father, The Lord Jesus Christ, and The Holy Spirit, and they work together as one God.

The Holy Spirit is God with us, and The Holy Spirit is inside of me, because I feel it, and I know it! And The Holy Spirit is inside you, too, if you have accepted Jesus Christ as your Personal Savior.

If you have not accepted the Lord Jesus Christ as your Personal Savior, right now is the time to do it. Because you do not have a promise of spending one more second, here in your body on this earth. You do not have a promise that you might get to take one more breath.

So, get right with God, before it is too late! If you do not feel God inside of your being, do not take for granted that you are going to Heaven. Pray right now, before it is too late, get right with God!

> *"Lord Jesus, I am a sinner, and I am sorry for all of my sins, and I ask You, Lord Jesus, to take all of my sins away, and come into my heart right now. I believe that You, Lord Jesus, have now taken all of my sins away, and You, Lord Jesus, now live in my heart. Thank You, Lord Jesus, In Jesus Name, Amen."*

Now, go in Jesus Name, and live for Him, and read your Bible. "The Holy Bible" is the inspired Book of God! And I believe every word of it. I have read it from beginning to end many times, and I live by it.

God's Word is Holy and God's Word is life, and God's Word gives life! I tell you to go and read "The Holy Bible" for yourself, and find out for yourself what promises God has made to you!

When you have accepted the Lord Jesus Christ as your own Personal Savior, you need to know for yourself what great, tremendous, powerful promises God has in store for you! Because God wants to bless you, and God loves you so much.

When you are God's child, you can now be sure that you are on your way to Heaven. And if you are a child of God, and you die before you wake up tonight, you will go to Heaven!

President Ronald Reagan was in office, in the spring of 1982, and I was in the hospital having my baby.

I had a real hard time during my pregnancy with Rachelle, and the contractions became stronger. So I was admitted back into the hospital, and I was not dilating. Then I was given more medications to force the contractions to be stronger.

After two days and nights the same specialist talked with Michael, as he stood next to the bed where I was in labor. He explained that this was one of the worst pregnancies that he had ever dealt with. And the baby had a good chance of being born dead, or dying shortly after birth, and I had a good chance of dying.

The medication that was causing the contractions to be harder for the past two days and two nights was causing me to get weaker, and I lost consciousness.

Then I saw myself looking down on my body. I was being put on another bed, and the bed with me on it was pulled through a hallway out into an elevator. Also, I saw a clear bag of medication connected to the bed with a tube going into my arm.

I saw the elevator stop, and I saw my body that was still lying on the bed. Then I saw people standing close to me. And I saw myself lying on a bed that had wheels on it, as it was rolled down a hallway into another room.

I saw my husband crying, and I saw myself floating upward on a cloud. I was in a bright light, as I was floating toward a ray of brighter light.

I had a feeling of contentment and peace, as I was floating upward.

Suddenly, I was being pulled backward, and then I felt pain.

I opened my eyes, and I heard Michael say, "Her eyes are open".

A doctor said, "I thought we lost you for good, for a while there".

Then I saw Michael dressed in blue hospital array, which allowed him to be in the delivery room with the staff that was taking care of me. Then Michael told me that we had a girl, and he was very excited, as he told me, "You had a girl, and she's alive".

And, I could just scream, and shout, and jump, and dance, because God is so truly good to me! God gave me a healthy, baby girl at 8:22 pm on April 25, 1982, and she is perfect.

There was never any water on her brain after she was born, and her body was perfect in size, and she weighed eight pounds, four ounces. Since we were surprised that God gave us a girl, instead of a boy that we were supposedly having, we did not have a name for her.

Then her sister, Mary Michelle, wrote on the chalk board in school that her name would be just like hers, Mary Michelle Proctor. We did not want their names to be exactly alike, so we came close, and we named her, Mary Rachelle Proctor.

Yes, Mary Rachelle was and still is gorgeous. And nobody could have ever been happier than I was. I am still happy to get the golden opportunity for God to entrust such a wonderful gift, as my baby girl with me. Rachelle is so perfectly made, and she acts just like me, they say.

Rachelle is absolutely a bundle of precious promises from God that I stood on for years. The love I have for my little Baby Rachelle is from God. I also love my other two children, Mike and Mary, as much as I love my little Baby Rachelle.

Mary Michelle holding Baby Mary Rachelle

Me (Mary) holding Baby Mary Rachelle

Mary Rachelle with me at an amusement park a few years later

Mary Rachelle playing ball

5—An Angel

Rachelle had just turned eleven years old on April 25, 1993. And her daddy had cancer surgery only a few days after she was born that saved his life, or she would never have gotten to know him.

We were blessed with the eleven years that my husband, Michael, got to be with us. Because the doctors and Michael always said that, if I had not insisted that he have a mole taken off his back, he would have died within a few weeks, right after Rachelle was born.

Rachelle was our miracle baby. We could have both died because of complications I had when I was pregnant with her. Because my husband and I were told that my baby would not be normal. If I insisted on carrying it, until after it was delivered, or killed us both.

Well, Rachelle was born, and she was perfect, and I got well. And Rachelle made Michael and my family of five complete, because Michael and I had two other children, Mike and Mary Michelle.

During the first years of Rachelle's life, our family lived in Eudora, Kansas, in a home that we were buying. I baby-sat in our home, so Rachelle did not have to go to a baby-sitter's house; while I worked at a bank full-time, or someplace else, like all the moms did that I baby-sat for.

Rachelle was raised in Assembly of God churches just like Mike and Mary Michelle. She asked The Lord Jesus Christ to take her sins away, and come into her heart and life when she was three years old at home in Eudora, Kansas, when I was baby-sitting.

Rachelle has always been the apple of my heart; because I was, always, truly happy that I was so very blessed to have this gorgeous baby girl.

The church had a big shower for Rachelle. Also, ladies let us borrow all kinds of things for Rachelle, including a beautiful, new, blue baby buggy that had to be given back after Rachelle got too big for them.

Wow! Did I ever have fun pushing Rachelle in the baby buggy. And Mike and Mary Michelle, also, went on walks with Rachelle and me. But, of course, they could only go on walks, and push Rachelle in the buggy when I was not baby-sitting. And, I only baby-sat for a couple of small children on one or two days of the week when Rachelle was real little; which was good, because I had a lot of time to spend with my children.

I pushed Rachelle in the buggy, and we went to the Eudora grade school. So all of the children and teachers, and, even the principal could see how beautiful Rachelle was, because we were very proud of her.

And, all of the children, teachers and principal looked at her in the buggy, and said "Wow! Rachelle is beautiful".

Of course, Mike, Mary Michelle and I grinned from ear to ear, because we were so excited about having a new baby in our family. And, Mike and Mary Michelle got to hold their little baby sister, when I took her to their classrooms, because it was show and tell day at the grade school.

Then, Rachelle got to go for a buggy ride all the way to the Eudora high school, on a Saturday when Mary Michelle had cheerleading practice, and Mike had basketball practice. It was a long ride for Rachelle in the baby buggy, all the way from their home to the high school, but she slept all the way there. Then, after we got to the high school, there were a lot of steps that I had to pull the buggy up, in order, to get inside the school gymnasium, where the practices were held for basketball and cheerleading.

I held Rachelle on my lap, all during the time, that I watched Mike and Mary Michelle practice their sports. And, while we were sitting there, my best friend, Alice, sat next to us, and watched Rachelle drink milk from her baby bottle, as I held her.

Then, when Mike and Mary Michelle were through with their basketball and cheerleading, they left with me. And we pushed Rachelle in the buggy back outside of the gymnasium, where we had a hard time keeping the buggy from rolling down the stairs too fast. But I held on, very tightly, to the baby buggy's handle. And I did not let the buggy get away from me, as I slowly went down each step, with Rachelle in the buggy.

Then, I pushed her in the baby buggy, as Mike and Mary Michelle walked next to me, when we crossed the streets. But they took turns helping me push the buggy with their baby sister in it, all the way home.

All during the time that I was pregnant, my husband worked and did any job he could get to pay bills. Then right after Mary Rachelle was born, Michael was diagnosed with melanoma skin cancer, and he had one surgery after another for three years, and then the cancer went into remission.

Then the doctors thought the cancer was gone because it had been in remission for five years, so I thought my husband was over the cancer. Things were going fairly well for us, and we got to have fun and go to places like Royals Ball Games in Kansas City, and Kansas University Games at Lawrence University College, and Mickey Mouse Ice Skating events, and Worlds of Fun in Kansas City.

Michael worked at Sunflower Army Ammunition Plant that was run by Hercules, where he worked taking down old buildings that had asbestos materials inside them. Then cut backs with state jobs caused that job to close, so Michael's stress level got worse.

It is making me cry so much, as I write about how hard my husband worked to provide for our family. Many times, I would tell my husband that I appreciated him, and I would tell him how good he was to our family.

Rachelle was only a few days old, when Michael was in the hospital having surgery for the first time, to have melanoma cancer removed from his back. Then, since I had our new baby, Rachelle, and two other children to take care of, Michael was not dismissed after two weeks in the hospital. Because we needed to have somebody that was qualified, and who could come and stay with us, to help me take care of Michael.

So my sister, Betty, came and brought her and Dave's little boy, Shawn, and stayed with us for several days. Betty was a nurse, and we appreciated her help with Michael, and everything else there was to do around the house, with a new baby in it.

Although, some of my adoptive family that lived closer to us, than Betty did could have helped me, they were not available at that particular time.

I was never adopted by my step-mom, and my dad had died several years earlier. So some close friends of ours in our church where Michael preached in Eudora, Kansas, adopted me. And that was when I was pregnant with my third child.

The people who adopted me were lonely for a family. And I longed to have a family that I could be around on a daily basis. I never thought there would come a time when Michael and I would not be in the ministry. And we lived too far away from my family to feel close to any of them any longer.

Larry and Peggy, people who wanted to adopt me, called and asked me to meet them at the Lawrence, Kansas, court house where they legally adopted me, when I was thirty-one-years-old, and I was married with two children, Mike and Mary Michelle. Peggy wanted to change my name to Latisha Wright Proctor, but because of all the trouble it would be to have so many papers changed, we decided not to change my name; however, she wanted me to learn how to drive so I could go places.

I did not have a driver's license, and I did not learn to drive for several years after my husband and I were married. Because when I was sixteen-years old my sister, Betty, and I went alone in my parents' car to get eggs. My dad told me that I could drive about two miles from where we lived in the country outside of Rankin, Illinois, to pick up eggs from a farm. And that was the only time I had driven without adult supervision.

Betty and I were friends, and she went with me, and since she was younger than I was. And I thought this would be a good time to practice driving 65 miles an hour, but there was fresh gravel on the old country road. We picked up a box of about five dozen eggs. And the eggs were in an open box on the seat between Betty and me. But instead of going straight home, I wanted to show some of my classmates that I was driving.

Well, after I got the eggs I drove a few feet down another fresh gravel road, and then I turned around in one of my classmate's driveways. I was beeping when I put my foot down on the accelerator, and I got the car up to 65 miles an hour real fast. But it started sliding on the fresh, gravel, country road. Then the car was going fast, and it was sliding. So I slammed on the breaks, and Betty and I started screaming, as the car zoomed out of control.

The car hit an electric pole, with a transformer on it that was off to one side of the road. And my head hit the window on the driver's side of the door, so the window shattered. And I thought Betty's brains were splattered all over me, because I forgot about all of the eggs in the open box, on the seat between her and me.

Betty was beautiful, and she had long, shining, blonde hair and big, blue eyes. She had always been skinny, and she was less than five foot tall. Her body was perfect, and Betty's health had always been good. At school I always tried to include her in my circle of friends. And if people did not respect her, they were not friends. But now, here she was in the front seat of our parents' car, and she was about to die with me.

I always felt like I was already dead, because of things that had been done to me in my childhood. It was an escape mechanism that I had taken on, to keep from losing my mind. So it would be no big deal to me to die in this car accident. But Betty was my precious little sister, and she deserved to live.

The car stopped after it hit an electric pole that had a transformer box attached to it at the top. That pole was wooden, and it was broken enough that it had to be replaced. So sparks from the high voltage transformer overhead were jumping around the pole, as the transformer hung by wires over the top of the car.

As the car hit the pole on the driver's side, Betty and the eggs on the seat between us, hit me on the right side of my head and arm. And my head broke the glass window on the driver's side, and I ended up on the floor between the steering wheel and the front seat.

I could not have gotten out of that car by myself, because I was totally wedged into a little area of the floor. And I was caught between the door of the driver's side and the steering wheel. The door could not be opened, because the door was wrapped around the electric pole.

Betty said that I was screaming, and I did not stop screaming, until I was out of the car. But I did not remember screaming after the accident. I only remember that I was standing a few feet from the car, and I just stood there looking at the flashing electricity from the transformer.

Betty got out of the passenger side door of the car with me. She did not look hurt, and her hair was flying around her face, and she was looking at me. I did not hear Betty say anything to me, as she walked toward me.

Then I saw that there was a light shining all over me. Then the light disappeared, and I just stood there without saying a word. And I saw Betty standing a few feet from me, and she was watching me.

I never knew how I got out of that car, but Betty seemed to know. Betty did not get hurt, and I have thanked our good Lord and Savior, for that many times.

I stood watching the sparks from the transformer over the top of the car, and it looked like the fourth of July. As the ground part of the pole was leaning away from the car, and the rest of the pole was leaning over the car. The part of the pole that was over the car touched the broken out window of both the driver's side and the windshield. The transformer was attached to electric lines that hung over-head, and that is where the sparks were coming from.

A car stopped along the side of the road, but the people did not get out. And I kept standing there watching the sparks over the top of the car. And at the same time, there was such a calm feeling that came over me when I first stood there with the bright light all around me. And now that the light was gone, I still felt calm.

It was a funny thing, because that light had been all around me, and I saw it because the light was on me. And I felt a warm, yet, cool breeze, and somehow, I felt like there was a glow coming from me, or that was part of me, but I did not think about anything.

The light was like a cloud covering over me, and I felt like it was part of me.

I know this might sound crazy to some people, but a friend of mine told me about that light one time. She said that one time she stopped her car along a country road, because there was a car wrapped around an electric pole.

Sparks were going into the sky from a transformer that was close to the top of that pole. So she was afraid to get out of her car, and there was no way for her to call for help from her car.

As she looked at the car wrapped around the electric pole, she saw an angel!

She said after she saw Betty open her door, and get out of the car, she saw an angel get out of that car with me!

Then she saw the angel standing next to me, as I was watching the sparks from the transformer!

My friend said that she had never seen an angel before in her entire life, until then, *but she knew, that she knew, that it was an angel*!

And that was why she kept staring at me, when I was standing there; which was not far from the accident that had just happened. She did not see my feet touching the ground, and the angel stayed with me for a few seconds. Then the angel disappeared, but she was positive that she saw the angel.

She described the angel, as looking like a picture of a guardian angel walking close to a child, as the child and the angel walk across a bridge.

She said there was a light all around the angel and me. And she saw the angel come out of that car with me on the passenger side of the car, and stay with me for several minutes. And she, also, saw the angel disappear.

If I died for even a few seconds in that accident, why did I feel so alive? I did not feel dead and gone any longer. And I felt no pain, and my body was not hurt from that accident.

I did not feel anything, and I did not see the angel, but my friend saw it.

What I saw, was the light that was part of me, at that time. And I felt the peace; and I felt the calm of the cool, but warm wind that was all around.

I still stood in that same spot where the light had shown all over me, as a man from a nearby farmhouse saw the accident, and he called 911. So the police came, and a fire truck and more people came.

Then I was back in the house, sitting on a sofa where my family lived, and Betty was right beside me. But I was in a daze, as Betty asked me, "Mary, are you okay?"

Betty was sitting close to me on the sofa, and she had her arms around me. Betty was concerned about me, and I almost killed her in the car accident.

I felt real bad about endangering Betty's life, but she was not mad at me. And I asked, "Are you okay, Betty?"

I did not have a driver's license, although my dad had given me permission to take the family car, and drive it without anybody that had a driver's license riding with me.

We did not go to a doctor to be checked out, and we did not have the money to buy another car after I totaled that one. So I stayed at an elderly man and woman's home that needed help for the summer. And I worked days at a drive-in restaurant, Steak'n Shake, to pay for another car for my parents.

Every time I thought about driving after that, the scene of the accident, and how close I had come to killing my little sister, Betty, would come to my mind. So I did not drive again for years.

6—RAPED

It was in June of 1957, and President Dwight D. Eisenhower was in office, when East Saint Louis, Illinois, received 16.54 inches of rain on June 15. At the same time Khrushchev was interviewed on US television, and the first US runner broke the four minute mile barrier.

And I was just a little kid, and I was promoted to an upper class for Sunday school that I saw an older, neighbor boy who was in the same Sunday school classroom that I was in.

I was very afraid of him because he raped me. He ruined my life, because he trashed me worse than anybody in the entire world could hurt me. I was actually terrorized of him, because he destroyed any sense of purpose that I could achieve in life.

I had horrific memories about how unmercifully he had conquered me. Although I did not have a choice about rather or not I should forgive him. Because in "The Holy Bible", it says that we forgive our debtors as Christ forgives us our debts. I wanted Christ to forgive me of my debts, so I had to forgive him for abusing me and raping me.

Even though, what he did to me, and how he went about it, conquered me of my innocence, and much of my happiness throughout the rest of my life.

My parents were the ministers of an Assemblies of God church in Indiana, where many teenagers came. And he was one of the teenagers that came to our church. He was also a young teenage boy, who lived with his family in an apartment that was part of a gas station that was next door to our home and our church.

How could he have, ever, imagined raping any little girl on her seventh birthday party the way he tortured and raped me?

My mommy trusted him because she did not know he would hurt anybody. So, she told me to obey him, and do what he told me to do.

If he complained to my mommy that I did not do what he told me to do, I would get a spanking. My parents did not tolerate any of their children to disobey, or they would get spanked.

He convinced Mommy that he could take care of me, and he would not let me get hurt. And he told my mommy that he could save my life, if I fell into the creek that was behind our house, because I did not know how to swim. He also told my mommy that his mom was burning trash next to our house, and he would make certain that I would not go around the area where hot ashes escaped.

He said if he was taking care of me he could tell me not to do something that would protect me from getting hurt.

So he got my mommy to let him take me out to play, and he horrendously hurt me. He also told me not to tell anybody, because I would get into trouble. And my parents would spank me real hard, because they would know that I was a real bad girl.

Then after he was finished with me, and I entered the kitchen, my mommy and two of my sisters, Linda and Betty, and, that teenage boy started singing.

"Happy birthday to you, happy birthday to you..." (Happy Birthday to You was written by American siblings, Patty Hill, and Mildred J Hill, in 1893, and the copy-write is now owned by Warner Chappell Music.)

My mommy, of course, did not know what happened to me. So, she was disappointed in me, because I was filthy when I came into the house, after he left me alone.

But he assured my mommy that I was okay, and he was ready for some birthday cake.

And, my mommy started laughing at him, because she must have thought he said something funny. And she turned her attention to the cake.

And, I just stood there in a daze. Because he just got through hurting me so badly that my head felt like it was broken. And he just got through raping me!

When my mommy gave me a piece of cake, I just looked at it. Then Mommy was busy with the cake, and everything else she had to do. And a few minutes later, my mommy gave me a little rake for my birthday, and she gave Betty something.

Mommy had this birthday party for my little sister, Betty, and me both, because our birthdays were only a couple of weeks apart.

My mommy was young, and very beautiful, and she prayed and sought God with all of her heart every day and night. She was a real good parent, and she was also a truly reverent wife to our dad.

She named me after her, Mary, and my grandma, Mary.

My mommy had exceptionally high moral standards. She did not even allow us children to say "gee", because that was too close to using the name of our Lord Jesus in vain.

It would have devastated my mommy. And I do not know what she would have done, if she would have ever found out how badly my head and brain were hurt by the teenage boy who went to our church, and what he did to me.

My mommy did not know he hurt my head and that he did anything bad to me. And I never told anybody about what happened to me on the day that Mommy had a birthday party for Betty and me, before I was even seven years old, because I was conquered.

Mommy had her hands full with us five little girls, Linda, me, Betty, Miriam, and Judy. And Mommy also had a boy named Eddie who only lived for about a day. And she had several miscarriages, because she was pregnant almost all the time, during her married life to my Daddy.

Me, Linda, Mom holding Judy, Betty, Miriam & Dad

Picture copyright William O. Fuller Palos Hills, Illinois: Model Release not obtained for subjects of photographs

7—Died

◇◇◇◇◇◇◇◇◇◇◇◇◇◇◇◇◇◇◇◇◇◇◇◇◇◇◇◇◇◇◇◇◇◇◇◇

Although the sun was shining, a breezy cold front was coming in on this November 12, 1958, Thursday morning, and Lake Village Grade School in Lake Village, Indiana, let the children go out to play after lunch.

So almost all of the children were outside playing, and some of them ran to the merry-go-round, and others ran to the new sliding-board, and a lot of them ran to play ball, and some of them had jacks and balls, marbles or jump ropes.

Running outside and down the concrete steps, I was yelling, "Wait, Kathy, I have a rope, and we can play with it, so stop and wait for me at the bottom of the stairs, and I'll give it to you!"

Kathy was my best friend, and she lived two houses away from our home. And Kathy and her sister, Joni, stood in front of our home to wait for the school bus every weekday. Joni was my sister, Linda's, girlfriend, and Joni and Kathy came to our church whenever their parents let them.

Linda, Betty and I were attending Lake Village Grade School, and I was in the third grade. It was recess, and most of the school kids were playing outside, and I was jumping rope to the chant, "Down in the Valley, Where the Green Grass Grows, There Sat Mary, As Sweet As, A Rose", author is unknown.

Then, I saw my big sister, Linda, sitting on steps that led to the school gymnasium, and she had her head down. And it looked like she was crying, so I ran out of the turning rope to see what was wrong with her.

Linda was crying so hard that her body was shaking, as she told me, "Some kids came up to me and said, 'Mommy died!' They said their mom called the school, and said she heard it on the radio".

I was very surprised at what my sister related to me, so, defensively, I yelled, "They're lying! Mommy didn't die, she's in the hospital".

After I said that to Linda, I hurried over to where some boys were talking to friends that I had been jumping rope with, and one of the boys said to me, "You're mom is dead".

I said, "Liar! My mommy is not dead, she's in the hospital."

Linda heard me yelling, so she cried harder, and then recess was over, so we all went back inside the school building.

Mrs. Arbuckle was my third grade school teacher, and her husband was the principal. I was afraid of him because everybody knew if you got into trouble he might spank you with a paddle that had holes in it.

I never got spanked, but sometimes I thought that I heard kids crying real loud, because maybe they were getting spanked. Now there was this principal who was talking to Mrs. Arbuckle, and they both looked at me, so I just knew that I was in trouble for calling somebody a liar, and then the principal went back out of my classroom.

My teacher did not look at me, so I focused on doing my school paper. And nobody said anything to me about what I had said outside at recess, and I hoped nobody would tell one of my parents that I had called somebody a liar, because my parents would spank me.

My mommy had told us, "If you get into trouble when you are not with Mommy or Daddy, you will get a spanking when you get home".

After my sister's and I got home from school that day, Grandma Mary Fuller was there, and she had clothes hanging on lines strung throughout the house. Then, she was taking care of more laundry. So she let me go to our neighbor's house to sell some Bibles and cards for a school project.

A man had come to school that day, and told everybody about Gideon Bibles. He said that anyone would get a Bible, if they sold boxes of cards and Bible concordances that were listed on a brochure that he gave to all of the school children.

I was excited about selling any of the items on the list, because I did not have a Bible of my own. And did I, ever, want a Bible of my very own.

So I must have spent hours trying to get somebody to buy something on the list. Because the woman and man who had the gas station let me stay outside of their business. And I ran up to every car and truck that stopped at the gas station, but nobody wanted to buy so much as a card. So, without any luck, after dark, I went back home.

As I walked back home from the gas station where I had been trying to sell Bibles and cards, I thought, "I bet Mommy and Daddy will buy some Bible things. As soon as Mommy gets home from the hospital, I'm sure she will want me to get a Bible, and she might even buy a Bible for herself".

The next thing I remember is sleeping on the sofa in our living room. Then Daddy came home and sat down on the sofa, and he was crying as he was talking to us three little girls, Linda, Betty, and I. And Daddy was telling us to wake up because there was something he had to tell us, and then he put his arms around all three of us girls.

I had been asleep, so I thought it was strange for Daddy to want to tell us something during the middle of the night. And I was rubbing my eyes, so I could try to see Daddy better. Then I looked at Linda, and I could see that she had been crying.

I thought, "Oh no, Mommy found out I called somebody a liar, and now, Daddy is going to spank me!"

I was so sleepy that my eyes could verily open to look at Daddy, and I did not know what he was going to do. Was Daddy going to have the principal spank me with the paddle that had holes in it?

I squinted so I could see Daddy better, and I realized that he looked like there were tears coming down his face, so I thought, "Was Linda crying because she was sick like Mommy?"

Daddy said, "Mommy died today".

I thought, "Why did you say that, Daddy? Mommy is in the hospital, and Mommy is coming back home".

Then, because Daddy and Linda were crying, they caused Betty to cry.

I thought, "Mommy won't like it because Betty is crying".

I did not cry, but I just sat and looked at all three of them crying.

At the same time that Daddy told us little girls that Mommy died there were two people who came into our house, and they tried to get us to go home with them.

Daddy said, "You girls can go home with these ladies for the night, and I'll come and get you in the morning, and you don't have to go to school tomorrow".

Linda said, "I want to go to school, and I like school".

I said, "I'll wait for Mommy to come home and tell me if I can stay home from school, because she always tells me when I can stay home with her".

I continued, "I need to stay here and wait for Mommy because she won't like it if we're gone when she gets home".

With that, Daddy lost it, and he left the room and cried. And he left us alone on the sofa to debate with those complete strangers. Then one of the women was trying to convince me that we should go to her house for the rest of the night.

She insisted, "Come with us, and we'll take you to our house. And you can decide what you want to do in the morning".

I could see that there was no getting out of having to leave our house, even though it was in the middle of the night. And it was cold outside, and Mommy would be upset if we were gone when she came home.

In fact, Mommy would be worried if we left without her because she would want to go with us to somebody's house. So I thought it would be a good time to try and bargain our way out of having to go with these people.

I said, "I will go with you, if you let us take a bath".

So they said that we could take a bath, and we went with them to their house. And they were very nice to us.

Then the next morning Daddy came and got us three little girls. And Linda still wanted to go to school, even though, Betty and I went with Daddy, because he said Betty and I could help him pick out a casket for Mommy. But, of course, Betty and I did not know what that meant.

We went to Michigan City, Indiana, where Daddy said the funeral would need to be, because Grandma Raska would have a hard time getting someplace that wasn't close, since she was in a wheelchair.

I was excited, as I asked Daddy, "Are we going to get to see Grandma and Grandpa, and are Grandma and Grandpa going to come to Mommy's funeral?"

I did not know what a funeral was all about. I only knew it was going to be something special that we were going to help Daddy do for Mommy.

I thought, "Oh good, when Mommy comes home from the hospital, she is going to get to see Grandma and Grandpa, and she will like that".

I remembered when we went to see Mommy's parents, and they always laughed, and Mommy was always so excited. But the last time we went to see Grandma Raska, she was in a wheel chair because her hip was broken. Then, we set on her front porch, and Mommy told Grandma about miracles that happened to her children.

Mommy was feeding my baby sister, Judy, and Mommy was excited when she talked. And Grandma was holding my baby sister, Miriam, on her lap, as she called me over to where she was sitting in her wheel chair, so she could hug me. And then she saw a red burn that went from one end of my inner lower right arm to the other end.

Grandma asked Mommy, Mary, what caused this burn? It's a bad one, that's for sure!

Mom told her, Mary wanted to iron, so I took the iron off the stove in the living room where I was ironing, and I let her iron. And I told her to be careful not to drop the iron because it was hot, so she picked it up, and it was too heavy for her to hold with one hand.

The next thing I knew, she had caught the hot iron with her right inner arm to keep from dropping it on the floor, and she didn't drop the iron on the floor, but the iron stuck to her inner arm. And smoke went rolling, and it's a miracle she didn't burn her arm completely off!

Grandma exclaimed to me, Oh, I bet that still hurts!

Then I shook my head up and down to let her know, it still hurts.

Mommy told Grandma, Mary irons her own clothes and Daddy's handkerchiefs. She is more careful now, because she has learned that the iron is heavy, and it gets very hot. So she knows not to leave it on the stove for too long.

I really liked to help my mommy. And I knew how much she needed all of us three girls to help her. I felt special to Mommy because I was named after her. And, of course, all of Mommy's children were special and loved by her.

The school bus picked us kids up right in front of our house, and most of the time all three of us little girls would sit together. I was proud of both of my sisters because Linda was so pretty, and Betty was so little and cute, also, both of my sisters were my best friends in school.

That was why I called a kid a liar when he said to Linda that Mommy died, although our parents taught us kids not to say bad things like that. But Linda was my sister, and nobody better, ever, hurt her because I knew that I would have beat every one of those kids up, if they would have hurt her feelings again, and nobody, better ever make one of my sisters cry.

I had not told Betty that the kids at school said Mommy was dead because she was too little to be involved in things like that. And I did not know where she was when Linda and I heard what the kids were saying about Mommy, because it was just the worst thing anybody had ever said to us.

It stuck in my mind like it was happening all over again, and every time I ever thought about it throughout the rest of my life.

Linda was very close to our mom because she was Mommy's first-born child, and she helped her all of the time, unless she was at school. When Linda was at home she helped Mom with the dishes, and she sat next to our mom when they read the Bible.

Although school was fun for Linda, it was hard for me. The first grade teacher told me to draw lines along dots, so I could write my name. But I had a hard time trying to figure out what she meant.

So it took me a lot longer to learn than Linda. For one thing, she did not miss school. Linda even went to school the day Daddy wanted us to help him pick out a casket for Mommy.

Betty and I both went with Daddy to help him pick out a casket for Mommy. So Betty and I got to sit in the front seat with Dad.

The only other time I remembered sitting in the front seat, was after I fell out of our car, and that had been about two years ago. And it was after we picked up a friend, Viola, to take her to a revival meeting with us.

Mommy was holding Miriam on her lap in the front seat. And we three girls and Viola were sitting in the back seat. Viola was kind to me, so she let me sit next to the door behind Mommy.

Then after we went a little distance down the gravel, country road from having picked up Viola, the door beside me started to come open. I grabbed hold of the handle to keep the door closed, but instead of the door staying closed, it flew open. I still had my grasp on the handle, so of course, when the door flew open I went with it.

Then I lost my grip on the door handle. And I fell on the gravel road with such force that it knocked the breath right out of me, as I was laying there for a few minutes.

My parents were screaming and praying, God, please don't let my baby be dead.

I was so stunned that I just lay still on the gravel road where I landed, after I fell out of my parents' car. I was lying on my chest that was bleeding.

And it felt like the burn that I got from our iron, the first time I learned how to iron Daddy's handkerchiefs. Then Daddy picked me up in his arms, and Mommy cried, real loud.

I saw myself being picked up by Daddy. And I saw Mommy crying.

However, I did not cry at that time, and, although I felt the entire front of myself burning, I did not cry, because I was in shock.

Daddy set me on the front seat of his car. And Viola took the baby from Mommy, who was hysterical and crying. So Mommy let me sit in the front seat between her and Daddy, as we continued on our trip to the revival.

Daddy asked Mommy, "Should we forget about the revival, and take her to the doctor?"

My parents prayed for me, so they knew that I was healed. They did not take me to a doctor; instead we continued to go to the revival church meeting that we were going to.

Mommy used a diaper to wipe off the gravel and dirt from my clothes. Then she let me wear her sweater, so nobody would see the bloody, torn dress I had on.

I never cried, and I did not talk. I just sat there feeling the hot pain in my chest.

Now, we were taking a trip to Michigan City, Indiana, to pick out a casket for Mommy, and we were not talking.

Betty was sitting next to the door, and I looked at the door handle to make sure she did not try to touch it, because I sure did not want Betty to fall out the door. Mommy would be very angry if anything happened to Betty.

I thought, "Don't worry, Mommy, I won't let anything happen to Betty".

At the funeral home Daddy was talking to a man. So Betty and I decided to have a look around the place, because we had never been in one place with so many flowers at one time.

There was a fancy casket with flowers on both sides of it, and the top of it was open. From where we were standing next to Daddy, we could see a man with a black suit on lying down in it.

Since we could still see Daddy, Betty and I went into the room to have a closer look at the man. And of course, we thought only a dead man would be in a casket.

But, we were wrong!

Betty and I were standing on our tiptoes looking into the casket at the man. And, Betty very quietly said, He has glasses on.

As soon as Betty said the man has glasses on, the man in the casket sat straight up. And Betty and I got scared to death!

So we both took off running, and screaming and crying. And of course, Daddy immediately came to our rescue.

But Betty and I saw that the man was following us. So we kept right on running and screaming and crying, as loud as we could.

And when we saw Daddy, we literally threw our arms around him, and we clung tightly to him.

The man apologized to Daddy, saying, I didn't mean to scare the girls.

Daddy was irate!

And he demanded, what is the matter with you? Their mother just died, and we're here to pick out a casket! Don't you have any sense, at all?

Then the man explained to Daddy, I was just seeing how comfortable the casket was. So I can tell people that I personally got inside the casket. And now, I can tell them it is quite comfortable.

Daddy was still upset. But he did not have to tell Betty and me to stay by him. We stayed so close to Daddy after that, you could not have put a nickel between us.

Betty and I clung to each other, on the way home in the car. We had not spoken a word, since the dramatic ordeal in the funeral home. I didn't, even, think about what Mommy would say when we got home.

However, Mommy was not at home when we got back. And I thought that was strange, because our mommy was always, either, at home or with us.

So Daddy let us three little girls help him pick out clothes for Mommy to wear to the funeral.

Mommy had a new brown dress with flowers on it that she had bought and worn once, and she looked pretty in it. And that was for Grandpa Fuller's funeral. That was also the first and only time, I remembered Mommy ever getting her hair fixed in a beauty salon.

Grandpa Fuller had died only three weeks before we were getting ready to have a funeral for Mommy.

Remembering all of that, I declared, Mommy will want to wear the new brown dress she wore to Grandpa's funeral. She looked pretty in it with her hair all curled and fixed. And Mommy will want to wear her watch, too, Daddy.

Then, I innocently asked, "Is Mommy at Grandma's house with Miriam and Judy?"

I did not realize Mommy had actually died. And I did not know what dying meant. I did not realize we would not see our Mommy again.

Then Daddy and Linda cried, and I thought they caused Betty to cry. But I did not cry, because I still did not understand what funerals really meant. And then Daddy gave me Mommy's watch to keep.

Mommy had explained it to me before I went with her and Daddy to a funeral one time. It was when a friend, Joyce, and her sister, Ilene's, mommy died, and my parents let me go to the funeral with them. Although I still had no comprehension about the final meaning of a funeral, and that somebody's life was gone from this world.

I had never been lonely before in my life. And I did not realize Mommy was not, ever, going to be here with us again.

I did not know about the changes it would have in store for our family, and how much it would change me.

That night Daddy and we three little girls spent the night at one of Mommy's sisters, Aunt Lil's, home with her husband, daughter and two sons. Then we went with Daddy to the Assembly of God Church in Michigan City, Indiana. And we saw the minister of this church where the funeral would be.

Then Daddy told a minister of that church that we did not have the money to pay for a funeral. And I could hear Daddy saying that Mary was not there anymore, and it will not be her in the casket, although it will be her body, but she is in Heaven.

Furthermore, I can't pay for a funeral. And I would never be able to come up with the kind of money to pay for everything like a casket. He was saying the funeral arrangement expected him to pay hundreds of dollars, just to have a casket with a body in it.

Daddy was saying, since Mary is not in that body anymore, her body could be buried anywhere.

So I could just bury her body in our backyard if it was up to me. But I know I can't do that because it might get me in trouble. And people might get mad at me, if I did that.

Besides, I know for sure Mary's parents and sisters and brothers would expect me to have a funeral for her.

So I could have one in our own church in Conrad, Indiana. But it would probably not be a good idea, because I don't want to disappoint her mother by not having a nice funeral for her. Furthermore, our church would not hold enough people to have the funeral there.

Daddy and the minister went on and on talking about having a funeral for Mommy, when she would not be there. And I did not understand what Daddy was actually saying to that minister.

However, when I overheard Daddy saying to the minister, Mary is not there anymore, and it will not be her in the casket. It will be her body, but she is not here anymore, she is in Heaven.

And I can't pay for a funeral. And I will never be able to come up with the money to pay for a casket. So I could just bury her body in the backyard, if it was up to me, because I don't have any money. So I can't pay for anything, and they want hundreds of dollars just to have a casket with a body in it.

I thought that I had it all figured out, even though it was all so confusing to me.

But after hearing Daddy talk to the minister, I just knew there was going to be a casket without Mommy in it.

I thought, no wonder Daddy caused Linda and Betty to cry, because Mommy was still alive.

Mommy was on a trip in Heaven. I should have known it all the time.

Mommy was playing a trick on us. Daddy was crying because Mommy was playing a trick on us.

She went on a trip without us, uh-ha! I figured something was going on. Well, I could go along about Mommy's acting silly with us.

And I thought, it's okay, Mommy, I know you aren't dead. I knew it all the time that you would not leave us, Mommy; you would never leave us, especially, Betty and your baby, Miriam, and your new baby, Baby Booties Judy.

I just don't know why you left Betty alone. And Linda and Betty have been crying and crying.

And I know you have Miriam and Baby Bootie Judy with you, because I haven't seen them, since Daddy let Betty and me stay out of school that day.

I kept on trying to figure out what was going on. "So, that's it, Mommy, you took them with you to Grandma and Grandpa's house.

You're probably mad at me for calling that kid at school a liar.

Well, I'm sorry, Mommy, I won't call anybody a liar anymore.

So, please, Mommy, don't be mad at me anymore!"

Then, I cried myself to sleep, on the front church pew.

The church people had a funeral for Mommy. And they really put on a show for her.

But Mommy did not come to the funeral.

Instead, there was somebody, or something in the casket that was in front of the church. And Mommy's brown dress with flowers on it was on that person.

I secretly whispered to Betty, "Don't cry, because that's not Mommy. Mommy never looked like that. But, I'll find Mommy for you".

Then I looked at all of the people in that church, because I was looking for Mommy.

And I just knew Mommy would want to be here, because there was her mommy in the middle of the isle in front of us, and she was sitting in her wheelchair. And there was Grandpa Raska. But he looked so different with a black suit on, and a white shirt on, and his hair was combed so different from the way I ever saw it.

I thought, I'm telling you, when Mommy hears about how much Baby Bootie Judy is crying, she'll come right up to us.

And Mommy needs to see how cute Miriam is in that pretty dress somebody put on her.

But Betty keeps crying. And Linda is screaming and crying so loud, that Grandma is crying with her.

"Mommy, where are you?"

I thought, "Mommy, why don't you come and get your little baby, Baby Bootie Judy? She won't take her baby bottle, Mommy!"

Everybody took turns looking at the casket. And then it was my turn.

So I was standing at the casket, looking at that person that was not Mommy lying there.

Mommy's sister, Aunt Lil, was beside me. And she picked me up, so I could see inside the casket better. Then she took my hand and my finger, and she touched my finger on the face of the person in the casket.

That's all I needed, because nobody could feel like a cold, old stone and be Mommy!

I just wanted, so badly, to yell out, "This thing in the casket is a cold, hard, old stone!"

Mommy never felt like that, my Mommy was always soft and warm, and Mommy always made noise!

Mommy would never leave her Baby Bootie Judy to cry like she was! And my Mommy would never stay away, and let Betty and Linda cry real loud, and make Grandma cry!

There was organ music that played from the time we entered the church, until we left the church. And I got so tired, of trying to get my mind off the organ music that I thought my head would explode, because it hurt so badly.

Then to top it all off, everybody at the church was mad at me. Nobody was smiling when I looked at them.

And everybody was hiding Mommy from me. And that was because I had called a kid a liar who made Linda cry.

So I looked into everybody's eyes, and saw how mad they were at me. Because they all gave me a bad look, and they all looked like I was in trouble.

All of a sudden, I knew why I was in so much trouble. And it was because of something I had never, and could never tell anybody.

I could hardly breathe, because I was so ashamed of what had happened to me, when I was still only six-years-old. And now I just knew that Mommy had found out that I was a disgrace, because that teenage boy had hurt me, and raped, so badly!

After that memory, I could not look into anybody else's eyes, because I knew why they were all mad at me.

Then I knew why Mommy left us. And I knew why Mommy left Baby Bootie Judy and Miriam. And I knew why Linda and Betty were abandoned. And I knew why Daddy had to be at the funeral without Mommy.

That teenage boy hurt me. And I was so sorry about that, so I never told anybody. And I would never, ever, tell anybody. Because I was ugly and I was dirty, and I was unlovable, and I needed to die!

After the funeral, we went over to Grandma and Grandpa Raska's house, and Betty stuck close to me. I knew Mommy was there, hiding from me, because I was so ugly, and I was dirtied for life. I now knew what a sinner felt like, I thought.

I wasn't noticed, as I slipped into a bedroom, where Grandma used to sleep. And it was where Mommy slept when we went to see Grandma. And I moved the shoes away from under the bed, so I could crawl way back under there where I would disappear forever. But my little sister, Betty, was right beside me.

So when I saw that Betty was next to me, I whispered to her, "Betty, please go away. I'm going to disappear, and nobody will ever see me again".

Betty whispered back to me, "No".

So, feeling all alone and sad, and feeling too sad to cry, I fell asleep, with Betty in my arms, under Grandma and Grandpa's bed.

When I think about the pain, I felt in my heart, I cry and cry and cry, because it hurts, so badly, all over again.

Mommy died, and I thought it was because she found out that the teenage boy had raped me!

I thought Mommy, and everybody, just knew what a bad, filthy, dirty little girl I was, and I always would be so dirty and ruined!

My mother, Mary Etta Raska Dill, died when I was eight years old, but I did not know that death meant we would never see her again.

Our family was torn apart, and my dad did his best to take care of us three older girls, Linda, Betty, and I. The two babies, Miriam and Judy, went to live with our Grandma Mary Fuller and her daughter, my Aunt Betty, until they were in school. Then Miriam and Judy came back home to live with Daddy and us three girls, Linda, Betty and me.

Linda, Miriam, Judy, Betty, & me (Mary)

Picture copyright William O. Fuller Palos Hills, Illinois: Model Release not obtained for subjects of photographs

8—Given up to Die

◇◇◇◇◇◇◇◇◇◇◇◇◇◇◇◇◇◇◇◇◇◇◇◇◇◇◇◇◇◇◇◇◇◇◇◇◇◇

Linda and Betty took care of me when I had rheumatic fever after Mommy died. Although, I did not know it then, however, they told me about it later on in life.

It was after we had moved from Conrad, Indiana, to the country not far from Lowell, Indiana. I was dying, and doctors had given up on me to ever get well. What little time I had left my sisters, Linda and Betty, gave their lives up for me.

Well, one spring day a tornado came, and we were alone because Daddy had to go out of town. And, of course, I was lying on the sofa in the living room, where I always was when I was not in the hospital because I had rheumatic fever, and my sisters could not move me.

We did not know anything about the weather, and we did not have things like a television, because that was a sin in our denomination. So when we saw a big black thing with a tail coming towards our house, and the weather went from no wind to a real lot of wind, and it got dark and hail started coming and breaking all of the windows out of the house where we were living at that time, us little girls, Linda, Betty, and I, got scared.

My sister, Linda, who was only thirteen years old started running up stairs for some reason, and a window that had never been opened, because it was stuck, flew open right as she went up half of the stairs. So that caused Linda to scream out in horror, and then I think she may have finished running up the rest of the stairs.

A lot happened during that tornado, and when it was over police came to our home. They asked Linda and Betty questions, and a newspaper editor wrote down what they said.

So Grandma Mary Fuller and Aunt Betty got the news about us three little girls being in a bad tornado that killed people and many animals. That was also how Grandma found out that many buildings and homes were blown away. And electric and telephone poles had the wires ripped off, and the poles and wires were blown away. Fences were blown away, and big trees were uprooted and blown away.

Since there was no way of contacting Daddy, except through the phone number of the place where Daddy worked, Grandma got that number from the operator and called. She was afraid we girls had been killed in that tornado, since several people had been killed. The news had our names listed and led people to believe that we three little girls had been left alone and died in the tornado.

The eye of that tornado must have been right over the house where we were living. Because so many of the trees and buildings, and black Angus cows, and fences and electric poles that were anywhere within miles of the house where we were living, were blowing in the horrific wind all around that house, with us little girls watching through the windows.

Even though, all of the windows broke out of the house, and glass was flying throughout the house, and the siding and a lot of the roof was ripped off that house, us little girls were not hurt. And our mommy's dog, Queenie, with her puppies in her little doghouse was not hurt.

The Holy Spirit was with us, and Jesus was protecting us. And when Daddy came home he was totally surprised to see all that had happened when he was gone. Because he was seeing what that tornado did for miles before he got to our house, not knowing that his family had been in the eye of that tornado that went through and around Lowell, Indiana, in the spring of 1962.

During that time, I was in and out of the hospital. And there was no schooling provided for me because I was given up on to die.

Then one day I could hear Daddy faintly saying for me to squeeze his hand if I could hear him. He heard of a tent revival that was going on several miles away, and people were bringing sick people there that were getting healed. If he could take me there, maybe, I would get healed from rheumatic fever. If I did not get healed and stayed sick, I would die and be with Mommy in Heaven.

The thought of getting to be with Mommy made me want to go, so I squeezed Daddy's hand. And he said that he would be in trouble with the law, if I died on the trip. It was too many miles for a doctor to let me travel without medical assistance.

But I just knew that I was already dead, so I did not care that somebody might say it.

Daddy, Linda, and Betty, and I went to the tent revival, and Daddy carried me out to the car, and laid me in the back seat on any pillows that they could find in the house.

And the last thing I remembered hearing Daddy say was, "Mary, you might not survive the trip".

Everything in my body ached, as I lay there in the back seat on the trip to that tent revival, and I would drift in and out of sleep.

At the church service, when the people that needed to be healed were all lined up in front of the alder, Daddy had me there.

The evangelist verily laid his hand on top of my head, and I was healed in Jesus Name. And I ran for a long time outside of that tent, and my sisters, Linda and Betty, were excited with me, and of course, Daddy was excited.

The next day, Daddy took me to the doctors who had been in charge of me for the time that I was eleven and twelve and had the rheumatic fever. And when I ran into the waiting room up to the nurse's window, she screamed like she saw a ghost. And the doctors were instantly on top of the situation, because they watched me run into their office, so they checked me all out, and said they could not believe it.

My heart was not swelled up and beating too fast anymore, and I was breathing normally, and I had the energy to run and play as most twelve year old children could. My blood count was normal, and I was told to do whatever activities I needed to in order to maintain my health, so I could go play.

One of the doctors, exclaimed, I believe in miracles and this is a miracle, and if I had not been taking care of Mary for all of this time, I would not be so excited, but she was dying, and now she is healthy, and Mary's heart sounds perfect!

Then I was asked if I had felt anything happen to me when I knew Jesus healed me. And I told the doctors, it felt like I touched the electric fence when I was real little, when we lived with angels who took my family into their little farm home, and took care of us, and fed us for a whole winter, and the angels are the Linderman family.

Then one of the doctors explained that my heart was so enlarged from valves not closing properly. In that all of the blood coming back to my heart was not entering my heart. And all of the blood that was in my heart was not leaving my heart.

The doctors continued that there was a dramatic heart murmur a couple of days ago. However, they did not hear any heart murmur when they were checking my heart at that time.

Although the doctors wanted to do a complete evaluation follow up of my heart, and they would need to admit me into the hospital for that.

After that a doctor took blood from me, and another doctor helped him give me such a complete physical that I had a hard time sitting still. I just wanted to run and play, because it had been a long time, since I had felt free of pain.

I was healed, and I knew it, and I just kept laughing, and saying, "I'm healed, I'm healed, Jesus, healed me!"

That was a real picker upper for our family, and we moved to Paxton, Illinois. So the doctors that took care of my health when I had rheumatic fever lost track of me.

We went to a new school, and the nurse got upset with me because I had never gotten any vaccines. And she told me, your mother and father do not love you, or they would have gotten you the vaccines that children get. I want to see your mother, and I want her to come into my office and see me in the morning.

That really hurt, because I still had a hard time believing Mommy was dead. I did not tell the school nurse that Mommy was gone, and I just looked at her when she said those mean things about Mommy.

Then I had to take my little sister, Miriam, to the school nurse because she got burned badly on a toy stove. And the nurse asked me why my mother did not come in to see her. But I did not answer the nurse, because it hurt me to talk about my mommy.

My baby sisters, Miriam and Judy, came to our house to live, after they had been living with Grandma Mary ever since Mommy died. And they brought all of their toys and clothes with them, so Betty and I had fun playing with them for hours upon hours.

Miriam was in the first grade and Judy was in kindergarten, and I would walk with my sisters to school. Then I would come home for lunch to get Judy, and walk her back to school for kindergarten.

Daddy would say it was a blessing because I went to the same school that they went to, so I could help take care of them. Judy would put her tiny hands into one of my pockets when it was cold, and I would walk with one of my arms around her, so she could walk closer to me. Then I would carry anything that we had with my other hand. And sometimes, it was so cold that I thought we would freeze to death before we got to school.

Then we would get to visit relatives in Indiana, our Aunt Miriam and Uncle Bob. And they had two daughters, Virginia and Diana, and because Diana was their youngest daughter she was the one who entertained my sisters, Linda and Betty, and I when we went to visit them.

Diana would let my sisters and I sit in little chairs at her little table. And we each got to hold dolls and have chocolate cookies and milk. Then Diana would let us play in her bedroom, and use her soft tissues to wipe our noses and faces off.

Diana's room and home were very clean and beautiful. Her bedroom smelled like perfume and flowers that I liked, so I thought for sure her family was very rich. And I wanted to be part of their family, so I could always be with Diana; because she was not only beautiful, she was also such a good friend.

Diana was too young to die. But she died in a car accident, when she was not much older than my big sister was. And we loved Diana, who was truly an angel, in Heaven with Jesus.

In order to get to be with Diana, I decided it would be better for me to die. So I took several prescription pills that a doctor gave to me when I had rheumatic fever. The pills were only supposed to be used for my heart. But I felt like my heart was hurt too much, for me to want to live anymore.

Well, I was sitting at my desk in Ellis Grade School where three of my sisters, Betty, Miriam, and Judy, and I attended after we moved from Paxton to the country outside of Rankin where my sister, Linda, attended high school, when I took the pills that I brought to school every day for the past few months. My best friend and sister, Linda, did not know about them, and I would never tell her; because I felt like my life was too sinful, to ever open up to anybody.

The only person who was in the classroom, when I took the pills was a friend, Kathy, and her dad was the custodian of the school, also, he was the bus driver.

I simply took the pills out of my purse, and put them into my mouth without any water. It was hard to swallow them, but I kept on clearing my throat, until they all went down. And they were dissolving in my mouth before I got them all swallowed, so the taste was awful.

Then within what seemed like a few seconds, I started feeling very tired, and my eyes became extremely blurry. So to keep from falling off my chair, I laid my head down on my desk.

I was almost asleep, when Kathy shook me to tell me to get up and go to the restroom; because a steady stream of blood was going down my legs. Then I saw a puddle of blood on the floor under my desk.

I was shaky, so Kathy helped me get up and go to the restroom. Then she said that she would get her dad, and he would clean up the floor and seat to the desk. And I needed to stay in the restroom, until her dad came to take me home.

Well, the custodian took me home, and I did not die, but I started menstruating, and we did not have a mother to explain things like that to me. Then my older sister came home from school, and told me it was part of being a woman.

But I missed Mommy so much that I probably cried a million tears, or more, ever since she died, and I just wanted to die and be with Diana and Mommy. And I thought about a man and woman that came to my parents' church, when I was a little girl.

It was when I was in our kitchen, and the woman came into the kitchen and got into a cabinet. And she got out mouse and rat poison, and she ate a spoon of it. Then when she was eating another spoon of it, I ran and told my parents and her husband at the same time, and they ran to the kitchen, and her husband grabbed the poison from her.

They started praying for her, and she just kept laughing, real crazy like. And she talked and laughed like a mean, scary, loud man. Also, she hit her husband and bit him, and she even growled real deep, and barked like a barking dog that was tied to a tree, that I had heard at a farm when my family lived with angels called the Lindermans.

I remembered my mom pushing me back out of the doorway to the kitchen. And then people in our church prayed and prayed, and they cast out demons in the name of Jesus, and commanded the demons to leave in the Name of Jesus. And they prayed for Jesus Christ to come into her heart and life.

Then I remembered how the woman acted, because she cried a lot, and then she prayed. That woman was about thirty years old, and she was pretty, and she combed her hair, and washed her face. Then she wanted to see the little girl that was in the kitchen, and my daddy let her see me, after they were all through with their praying, and she had washed herself and combed her hair.

Then she talked with a kind, quiet voice, and she smiled and said she was sorry for eating the mouse and rat poison in front of me. And she said that demons were in her for a long time, and now there were no more demons in her, and she was free. And she said that she asked Jesus to take all of her sins away and come into her heart.

But after I thought that I would just get real sick, if I ate some rat poison, I decided not to poison myself to make myself die. And, no matter, how much I wanted to be with Diana and Mommy, my little sisters and Linda would probably miss me, if I was dead.

Then not long after that Linda went to live with Grandma Mary Fuller. Then by the time Linda came back home, Daddy had gotten married again, and it was not long before Linda got married. So Linda moved out of our house where we lived with our new young mom, Flossie, and her beautiful little girl, Debbie. Then it was not long before my parents had my hearts delight, for my cute little baby sister, Joy, was born. Then my precious, baby brother, Jimmy, was born, so that gave my parents a total of eight children.

9—Angelic Beings

I t may have been my imagination, or that sometimes I prayed and sought God more than usual, that I sometimes had dreams. And, sometimes I envisioned the image of Christ or a type of person from my imagination, or something that was not touchable. Because I would see glimpses of angels and Angelic Beings that loved people and me, so much that they were for us and not against us.

I would be praying, and feel the presence of The Holy Spirit from within my body. Then I knew God was with me, but there were other times, I would pray and feel nothing. So I would start reading God's "Holy Bible" more. That's when I would really feel God's presence, all over again; because "The Holy Bible" is God speaking to people.

Jesus taught people to come to Him, and that everything Jesus taught was totally from God, His Father. Then after Jesus Christ was crucified and rose from the dead, He was taken up to Heaven to be with God, His Father our creator. And The Holy Spirit came as a Helper to people, so they would be drawn to God and truth. The Trinity is God the Father, Jesus Christ our Lord and Savior, and The Holy Spirit, and all three of them work together as one God.

The Holy Spirit gives people the power from within, and helps them discern right and truth in all things. The Holy Spirit draws people to God, and it is the Holy Spirit that causes people to feel God's presence. It is The Holy Spirit that causes me to feel God's presence and know that God is near.

I would see a glow that was a shining light in people's faces, as they prayed and sought God. And I knew that it was The Holy Spirit shining through them. Sometimes, I could see that glow around my children when they were growing up.

When my son, Mike, was very young, maybe around seven years old, he was baptized by his daddy, Michael, the minister at the Assembly of God Church in Eudora, Kansas. We believe in total submersion into water, and when he was coming up out of the water from being baptized, I saw such a glow all around him.

I prayed for my little boy, Mike, that God would always be with him, and use him. Also, I prayed that Mike would always be completely surrendered to Jesus, so that my son would feel Jesus close to him. And that my son would pray to Jesus daily to forgive him of any trespasses, and sins that he might ever commit. Then I prayed that Mike would have the assurance from The Holy Spirit of God, that he was accepted, totally, without blemish by our Lord Jesus Christ and Savior.

When Mary Michelle was around seven years old, she was baptized in the water baptistery at the Assembly of God Church. She was asked to make a public confession of The Lord Jesus Christ. And she said, "I have accepted the Lord Jesus Christ into my heart. And I believe that Jesus Christ is the Son of God and that He has taken all of my sins away".

Then I could feel the Holy Presence of Jesus, as the minister completely submerged Mary Michelle under the water. As he baptized her in the Name of the Father, the Son and the Holy Spirit, and he said that Mary Michelle was buried in baptism, and raised in fullness of life to live with Jesus.

The Bible says in Romans, chapter 6, being baptized was that she was buried with Jesus, when she was put under the water. When she was raised up from the water, it was as Jesus Christ was raised up from the dead by the glory of the Father. And that meant she walked with a new body in Christ Jesus, who is our Lord and Savior.

I prayed, Lord Jesus, please, always help my little girl, Mary Michelle, and watch over her, and give her comfort and health. And, please, always protect my little, Angel Mary Michelle, from any harm that comes her way. Thank You, Lord Jesus, for drawing my little girl to You; please, help her to always pray every day, and ask for Your Forgiveness for any sins that she does, and please, use my little girl and help her feel Your Presence.

Then I prayed, Lord Jesus, I am so unworthy in your presence. Please take any and all of my sins away that I have and will ever commit, because I am such a sinner, and I do not deserve any goodness from you or anybody else. I am so ashamed of all the sins I have ever committed, and I do not ever want to be a sinner. Lord Jesus, come into my heart and life.

Oh, how I wish that I did not sin; because I hate it when I am tempted, and I give in to any sin. I commit all that I do into Your Hands, Lord Jesus. Lord, help me to be good mother to your children that you have placed in my care, Thank You, Lord Jesus, my Savior and my Lord.

It felt like the love of God, and forgiveness from God, and Holiness about the presence of God was all around me. And I asked Jesus Christ to take away all of my sins, and to come into my life when I was only three-years old. However, many times throughout my life I had sinned, and gone back to Jesus, and asked Him to take my sins away and come into my life; because I felt like sin was in my life.

I did not want sin to keep me out of Heaven when I die. So I would pray again and ask Jesus Christ to forgive me, because I have a real conviction about sin when I do it. I sin often, but I go right back to Jesus, and ask Him to forgive me of my sins then come into my heart and life, and help me not to sin again.

It says in "The Holy Bible" that all have sinned and come short of the glory of God, and that means me. I have sinned, and I do sin, but I am ashamed of my sins. So I go to God in prayer and ask for His forgiveness from my sins, and I ask Him for help; because I need help from God every day, for I cannot make it on my own.

When our son, Mike, was eleven years old and Mary Michelle was eight years old, and our new baby girl, Rachelle, was only a few days old their daddy got sick. And I was starving myself, because I was on a diet to try to lose the weight that I had gained, while I was pregnant with Rachelle.

I wanted to get back down to the size I was before my baby was born. However, it took time, and it was hard to keep from eating, because I was so hungry. But I still fixed all of the meals and sat at the table, and took tiny portions of food on my plate.

Michael would tell me that I only had a month or so, to lose all of the weight that I gained, after each one of our three babies were born. If I was not skinny, I would have to find someplace else to live, and he would turn my babies against me by telling them that I was a hoar, and I did not want them. That always scared me to death! (I was not a hoar, but somehow, he would convince everybody that I was. People would believe him because he was a preacher.)

When Michael first started feeling worse, Mike graduated from high school. So my sister, Betty, and her husband, Dave, and their son, Shawn, came and helped me put on a banquet in honor of Mike for graduating. Then after the banquet was over, Mike and Mary Michelle went back with Grandma and Grandpa Proctor, and their Aunt Jeanie to visit relatives in Danville, Illinois.

Then when we went to Danville to pick up Mike and Mary Michelle, Michael pressured me to sell our home in Eudora and move to Danville; because that's where the Proctors lived, and other relatives lived on both my husband's side, and my side.

I did not want to move away from Eudora, but for the past several months every time we would visit family in Danville, part of our family would beg for me to move there. However, I did not want to move back to Illinois, because I liked living in Kansas, and we had a lot of friends, and I had a nice business baby-sitting.

Since Michael wanted to live close to his family, and we lived in Kansas, for nineteen and a half years, I thought about it. Of course, I prayed a lot, so I felt like he deserved to live close to his parents because he was sick; and he had melanoma cancer that was on his skin for three years.

Then it was in remission for five years, and now it had come back, only this time, the cancer was on his liver. And that was scary, because I loved Michael.

I decided if it was God's will for us to move to Danville, I wanted God to show me. And I decided that our home in Eudora meant so much to me that I wanted all of the money we put into the home back, and all of the money it cost to live there back. Then I would know that it was God's will for us to sell our home, and move to Danville, Illinois.

We had friends that went to our church who were in real estate, so I asked them to come over, at different times, and give me information about how much our home was worth. However, the amounts they both told me was not what I thought my home was worth.

So after having my children kneel and pray with me beside my bed, I told Mike to get a cardboard off the back of a tablet that was in the phone book drawer, and write "For Sale by Owner" and our phone number on it. Then he could put it on the tree in front of our home.

Although it was work, it was not long before I sold our home for what I thought it was worth. Then we needed to immediately get another home to live in.

And that was, definitely, God's will for our life.

Michael did not feel good, and I completely lost my voice when we looked at homes in Danville with a realtor. However, things worked out well for us, and we found a home that was exactly what I wanted. Although, it was way out of our price range, and the realtor was embarrassed to even present the offer to the owners.

We had to go back to Eudora, because I had to be there for my baby-sitting job in our home. Then right after we got home the realtor called, and said the owners accepted our offer; even though, it was ridiculously low for what they wanted. So, it was God's will for us to get that home.

Although Rachelle did not want to move from the only home she had known since her birth, she helped me pack her toys. She was only seven years old, and all of her friends were in Eudora. And Rachelle truly liked the school she got to attend, and it was within walking distance from our home.

On the day that the moving truck arrived, Michael was scheduled to have melanoma skin cancer surgery on his liver. And he insisted that I stay, and get our stuff loaded on the moving truck. So Virgil and Chester, and some other friends from our church in Eudora were with Michael for the surgery, as the men from the moving company loaded our stuff onto the truck.

I was truly concerned for my husband's health, because I wanted to be with Michael during the surgery. Although, I did the work of helping decide what went on the truck, and I finished packing, while I continually prayed for my husband. For I knew ever since I was a small child that I could always depend on God to take care of everything, and God would always take care of Michael.

Well, after Virgil and Chester came to our home with good news about the surgery, later on that night my husband surprised me when he came home. Because he left the hospital in Kansas City, walked to his car that was parked over two blocks away from the hospital, and drove himself all the way home.

Michael had two catheters draining fluids from his surgery, and he had come home to take over my position of being in charge of the move. He was on strong antibiotics, so he had strong pain medication in his body. Of course, I was very concerned when Michael arrived home the same day after his surgery, because he could have had an accident.

The hospital called, and they were truly upset, because they had been looking for Michael. They did not know he had just come into the doorway of our home, and we lived over 35 miles away from that hospital, and Michael had not been dismissed.

They were going to send somebody to our home to get Michael and bring him back to the hospital, because there were tests that he needed to have. However, he let them know that he would go back to the hospital, after he helped his family move to our new home in Illinois.

So Michael helped us move, with the catheters draining fluids from his body. He was very happy that we were moving to be close to our relatives, and especially close to his parents; because Michael and his parents were always very close.

Right now, I pray for these families, and friends that my family and I spent time with in Kansas, and I love every one of these people. And I know You, Lord God, love all of these people that I knew in Kansas, You, Lord God, also, love all of Your Children throughout the world.

Thank You, Lord Jesus, for allowing us the golden opportunities to minister to these people, and I know that it was only through Your Word that we knew what to do and how to minister to these Your Children. And I pray that You, bless these, Your People. And help them to feel Your presence, and may You, Lord God, be praised at all times by all of Your People, and that others see You in their lives, as well as, in my life. I give You, Lord God, the praise due You, forever and forever.

I prayed and pleaded with God to, please, heal my husband, because we needed him, and I loved Michael. And I could not raise our children without him, because my husband had convinced me that without him I would be homeless and have nothing.

I never thought about life without Michael, and he wanted to be alive, and take care of us, his family that he loved very much. And he would go to doctors in Danville, Illinois, and have more surgeries, again and again.

Michael was afraid to die, because he thought God would punish him for being too mean of me. But I would tell my husband that God does not punish people, after they die and go to Heaven. God forgives all sins anybody commits, and God never brings those sins back to His children.

God knows nobody is perfect, and nobody can be perfect. That is why Jesus came into the world, to forgive people of their sins, and the things Michael did to me, and said to me might not have even been sins. Michael was and is the daddy of my three children, and I had, and would always dearly love him and protect him at all costs.

This book is not about how I was abused, it is for healing to my mind and body. And I have prayed, and sought my Lord and Savior for years about how I need to let The Holy Spirit help me write my book.

For, everybody has been hurt throughout the years. And we all need to do as Christ taught us to do. That is to love one another as Christ loves us, and lay down our lives for one another.

Everybody has hurtful memories that can be used to destroy their loved ones and themselves. But the only way anybody can feel the peace, and love of God's forgiveness, is to forgive people who have hurt them.

It says in Philippians 4, in "The Holy Bible", to meditate on these things that are praiseworthy and of good report, and that are pure and lovely, for God will give you peace. And it says to learn to be content, in whatever circumstances you are in.

And back in Philippians 3:12-21, "The Holy Bible" tells us to forget those things which are behind. And reach toward those things which are ahead, for our citizenship is in Heaven with The Lord Jesus Christ.

The enemy will use your hurtful memories to take the joy right out of your mind, and this will ruin your health, and keep you from being happy.

If you are willing to let Jesus Christ help you have healing from your hurtful memories, *believe you me*, a real, big burden will be lifted off your mind and body that the enemy and destroyer used people and circumstances for to completely destroy you. Or at the very least, has tried to destroy you, and everything that you have tried so hard to succeed in.

And, that is exactly what the enemy almost conquered me with, every time I sat down and started writing "Abuse, Conquered, Alive", because I was hurt, and I would write about my hurtful memories. And it would destroy all of the beauty and goodness that could possibly come from writing this book. And I would dwell on what I was writing, and stay awake at night thinking about all of the hurtful memories.

Then of course, it caused me to shed many tears, and cry out to God.

Why, God, why did I have to go through pain and suffering the way I did in my life, so many times?

Why didn't I have a wonderful, pain, free life, like so many other people in this world have that are rich, and beautiful, and famous?

Why didn't I get to have my mommy live, and be there for my cute sisters and me all the time, instead of her dying, and us children living for so many years without a mommy to love us and take care of us?

And, why did I have to go through so much sickness, and be a burden to my family that loved me so much?

Then I would open God's "Holy Bible", and seek for answers to all of my questions. Because there was nobody in this whole, wide world that I could really, and truly, confide in about all of the hurtful things that happened to me, throughout my life.

Why wasn't there anybody that I felt confident in enough to talk to about everything, and anything that was hurting me, and destroying my peace of mind and my joy?

Because, people like to be the first ones to tell somebody else, and nobody, and I mean nobody; nobody needs to have anybody tell somebody else about your hurtful memories, especially the whole town, that just loves to hear and talk about people.

And, I studied God's "Holy Bible", so much that I got answers for my own hurtful memories; and everybody has hurtful memories.

And God wants to bless everybody, and prosper everybody, and replace everybody's hurtful memories with joy that cannot be taken away by anybody or anything, especially, hurtful memories.

Everybody can go directly to Jesus and talk to Him about anything.

Because, guess what, Jesus already knows all about everything.

No matter, how big or small anybody might think it is, Jesus has been waiting all of your life for you to, simply, come to Him and tell Him all about anything.

Jesus loves you, so much, that He will always listen to every single thing that you want to tell him. And He has all the time you want to give Him, to listen to everything, and He wants to listen to you, because Jesus owns you.

You are not your own, Jesus bought you with the highest price that, absolutely, nobody could ever pay for you.

This is how important you are to Jesus, because Jesus died for you and your sins.

When you ask Jesus to take away all of your sins, and come into your heart and life, He does right then and there, no matter where you are. And you do not need anybody to help you become a child of God, except, Jesus, and He will never turn you away.

And, once anybody has asked Jesus to take their sins away, and come into their heart and life, He does. Then you belong to Jesus, and then you become an adopted child of The Only Living God, God Himself, that's what it says in "The Holy Bible".

That is such a healing from my memories, and if you can, you need to read "The Holy Bible" for yourself. If you cannot read, listen to "The Holy Bible", and you will know that life is, actually, very short, and after you die it is forever and all eternity.

Where you choose to spend eternity is up to you, because there are only two choices, Heaven or Hell. Jesus is in Heaven with God His Father, and God is your Heavenly Father, after you decide to let Jesus come into your heart, because you are a child of God when Jesus lives in your heart and life, and you are adopted into the Kingdom of Heaven.

That is one of the reasons you want to live like Jesus taught people to live, after you have asked Jesus to take your sins away, and come into your heart and life. Jesus will change your mind, and you can be very, truly, sure that Jesus will always be your very, very, closest and best friend. And Jesus will always be right there with you, no matter where you are. And Jesus has left The Holy Spirit right here with you, to help you and listen to you.

The Holy Spirit comes into your heart and soul, after you ask Jesus Christ to take all of your sins away, and come into your heart and life. The Holy Spirit lives inside of you, after that, and The Holy Spirit helps you want to read and listen to "The Holy Bible", and understand it. And if you do not want to read it or listen to it, you do not want to condemn yourself or anybody else for that.

Sooner, or later, you will come to a place in your life, when you, finally, realize that nobody is here for you. And then, all there is left for you to do is to turn to Jesus, and ask Him to forgive you for not reading or listening to "The Holy Bible".

The Holy Spirit will help you understand what God is teaching you in "The Holy Bible", and never forget that Jesus is waiting right beside you, to welcome you back to talk to him.

Jesus has been watching you, and listening to, absolutely, everything that has been going on with you all of your life, and he certainly understands how much the enemy has been hurting you. Jesus conquered the enemy for you at Calvary, and Jesus has blessings waiting for you.

Jesus has been conquering the enemy that wants to destroy you, or that has already destroyed everything that you have ever tried to do. But do not give up, and do not fear any longer, for Jesus will never fail you.

It has been the enemy that has been against you, all this time, not Jesus. Jesus is the answer for all of your life, and all you need to do is go, and ask Jesus about that, Jesus will never fail you.

Why do you think Jesus died on the cruel, old, rugged cross for you?

It is because Jesus loves you and Jesus died to make a way for you, to have complete joy, and forgiveness from your sins. Because it is sin, and other people's sin that conquers you of your happiness and joy, and peace of mind. And it is sin that causes you to have hurtful memories.

Let Jesus erase those hurtful memories, and replace them with joy, unspeakable, and full of glory. If you will, please, just let Him, Jesus wants to bless you, because Jesus loves you more than you can, ever, in your entire imagination, ever comprehend.

Let Jesus take all of your hurtful memories, completely, away from you. And let Jesus replace all of your thoughts and mind, with the perfect and wonderful, complete, peace and joy that He wants for you, in your mind and body, because Jesus paid the price for you.

Right now, cry out to Jesus, for complete peace, and assurance that He has always been right here with you, at all times, Jesus has never left you.

It is you that have never, laid down, your hurtful memories, at the cross of Jesus. Oh, how Jesus wants to bless you with complete, wholeness of joy, unquenchable, and love you.

Jesus loves you, and nobody else has to love you, when Jesus loves you, because when Jesus lives inside of you. Jesus is all you truly really need, because then you are a child of God.

That will help you to love other people, even though, you have been hurt so badly, that all of your memories are of hurtful stuff that people have done to you.

Hurtful memories are big, really, big baggage that you carry with you everywhere you go, and they seep out when you least expect them to.

And other people's hurtful memories seep out onto your stored up hurtful memories. Until all of those hurtful memories of yours and theirs, poisons both of you. And you both end up with more hurtful memories that often, completely, destroy both of you.

So you feel like all you have are hurtful memories, piling up on top of you, until, the enemy uses your hurtful memories to completely destroy you, and everything you have ever tried to do. Now, you don't need that, *do you?*

My friend, I also love you, and I am crying so many tears, as I write my book, "Abused, Conquered, Alive"; because I have carried so much anguish around inside of me for almost all of my life, too. And I want so very much for Jesus to wipe all of my hurtful memories and your hurtful memories away, and give you such a peaceful, joyful heart, and memories that bring such a satisfying healing to your mind and body.

Won't you pray with me right now, "Jesus, here I am, I have been hurting, so very badly, for what seems like my entire life. And I can't stand it, because all of the painful memories that have been piling up, ever since

I was a little child, hurt me too bad, and I can't go on like that. So, please, take all of the hurtful memories out of my mind and body, and replace them all with Your Wonderful Peace and Love, Thank You, Lord Jesus".

You alone, Oh God, are good, and I am nothing without you. I will get my Bible, your "Holy Bible", and open it and read it for myself. And if I cannot read it, I will pray that you will send somebody, or give me something to listen to, so I will understand everything that you are saying in your Holy Words of Life in "The Holy Bible".

This is why I know that "The Holy Bible" is from You, Oh Lord my God, because look at how long these Holy Words have been around on the earth, thank You, Jesus, for saving my soul.

I feel your love and power, Lord Jesus, and I know that you will help me go on with my life, because my life is in You, Lord Jesus. I will only dwell on Your Holy Words that are written in Your "Holy Bible" from now on, and I refuse to let the enemy destroy me any longer.

I am the temple of The Living God, and God dwells inside of me. I sing Hallelujah; thank You, Jesus, and I Praise The Lord!

Oh, how I love You, Jesus, and I thank You, Jesus!

Wow! I don't know about you, but I feel the presence of my Holy God and Savior! Glory to God in the Highest, and I sing praises to Your Name, Oh Lord my God!

When the tempter puts hurtful memories into your mind again, let your mind scream out, "I know who you are, hurtful memories, so get behind me Satan, for you are not welcome here any longer! I am the temple of The Living God, and God dwells inside of me! No hurtful memories are welcome here anymore! I only want Jesus, and the Holy Words of God that are from "The Holy Bible" to dwell in my memories, because I am no longer a slave to hurtful memories."

Hurtful memories enslave you to destroy you. And those kinds of memories will destroy you and everything you do, until your health and mind are completely gone. Then all you are is a slave, because you are a slave to destruction from the enemy. And it is your decision to either let yourself be a slave to hurtful memories, or leave them all at the cross of Calvary.

Please, do not do what I did for most of my life, because I let myself be in bondage, and be a slave to hurtful memories, and I no longer am a slave. I prayed the prayer that I asked you to, please, pray with me, as I wrote it. While, I cried so much that I could not see straight, and I was letting my Lord Jesus guide me to help you, become free from being conquered by hurtful memories.

Look at some of the men in the Bible, even, King David did things that were not right, and he was a man after God's own heart. When anybody asks Jesus to forgive them of their sins that is, exactly, what Jesus does. And Jesus forgave Michael and me both for our sins. Just like Jesus forgave King David for all of his sins, and Jesus forgave Jacob for all of his sins in the Bible, and he became Israel, because Jesus forgives sins, and we all sin.

10—THE FIGHT TO STAY ALIVE

It was May 6, 1993, President Bill Clinton was in office, and Space Shuttle Columbia landed after Mission Number STS-55. Columbia was the shuttle that disintegrated over Texas about ten years later, which was on February 1, 2003, and it was on May 6, 1993, that Rachelle watched as her sister and mommy tried to keep her daddy alive.

Rachelle was thin, with long, blond, straight hair and big, blue eyes, and her cheeks were pink most of the time because she had fair skin, and she was healthy. She was an A student, and played a clarinet. She also played girls softball, because her interest in softball came from watching lots of games her daddy and brother played. And her daddy had not only played softball, he also coached a lot of games.

Rachelle's daddy was a Pentecostal minister, and he had changed, and he was sick and depressed often, because he had melanoma skin cancer that had entered his internal organs.

Michael used to laugh real loud about jokes he must have made up, and the way he said things, and did things with Rachelle's help were fun for them. And she stayed with her daddy where her family lived in Danville, Illinois, while I went to college to get a Bachelor of Science degree in nursing, until her daddy was losing reality due to cancer eating away at every organ that was in his entire body, so his personality changed, and he looked different, too.

It caused his brain not to work like it normally would have, so Rachelle's daddy might think something was not what it really was, or he might think one of his family members had something that he wanted, or both at the same time, and of course, this was very sad for a little girl. If I wasn't going to nursing school, and learning all about how people react in different illnesses and to different medications, it would certainly be frightening for me, too.

Although most of the time Michael was still able to relate to our little daughter, Rachelle, the way he used to, he was becoming more and more stiff and ridged. He had lost weight and his eyes took on a stare-like glaze, and instead of his skin being all tanned it had turned pale.

He was walking with a shuffle, in that he did not lift his feet when he walked, instead he just scooted his feet like some people do when they have a disease like Parkinson's. And when he walked up and down stairs he stomped his foot on each step, in such a way it made a louder than usual thump sound, and of course, this was not the way her daddy had always been.

Michael was in the care of hospice nurses by then, but the reality of what was going to happen never really entered our minds. All of our family, and that definitely included me, Rachelle's mommy, thought he was going to get well someday, and everything was going to be back to normal, as much as possible.

I was looking forward to the end of this semester, because I would be at home with my family for the first time, since I started going to college three years ago. The only reason I was going to college and studying all the time was because I had to get a job and support our family, or we would become homeless.

Michael and I both planned that I would work this summer, however, it was before the doctors signed Michael up with hospice. Ever since my wonderful husband, the father of our children, Mike, Mary Michelle, and Mary Rachelle, had been diagnosed with melanoma cancer he was on the fight of a lifetime to stay alive. I could not imagine life without Michael, and there was no way I would ever give him up to die, while I was still alive.

If we could somehow get by without me working, I would be able to stay at home, and be available to both Rachelle and her daddy, and our other children, Mike and Mary. I was praying as often as I could, for my husband to get well, maybe, all he really needed was for me to be at home with him, like I always used to be.

I just knew that a big miracle would happen for my husband, Michael, and he would be instantly, completely healed. Many people had been praying for him, throughout these eleven years he had been battling with cancer, and I prayed a real lot for my husband, whom I dearly loved so very much.

I believed that Jesus was going to heal Michael, and the sooner that would happen, the better, because we had been married for over twenty-two years. And I was in complete subjection to my husband, because he had convinced me that I could not live without him, and I did not ever intend to live without him.

I did not know anything about our business affairs, because Michael was not only the boss, he controlled everything that had to do with our lives. My husband also planned to outlive me, because he had plans for how he was going to live his life after I died. And I thought that God was going to take me to Heaven long before my husband went.

Michael used to want people to be around him almost all of the time, however, for the past few months melanoma cancer had been causing him to be in constant pain. Consequently, Michael would sit in a stiff position to try and not move, so his body would not hurt quite as much, because every movement caused his body to hurt with excruciating pain, and sometimes he even tried to explain to me how the pain felt.

My husband would tell me that the pain hurt, so badly, that he could not stand it, and his entire body hurt to move.

Michael would yell at me that the pain was like, "How would it feel, if I put my fist through your head".

Of course, he meant my head. But he never put his fist through my head because I always ducked, or I would not be alive to write my book, "Abused, Conquered, Alive.

11—CONQUERED

In our ministry and daily lives we read "The Holy Bible". Which tells us that Jesus Christ came into the world, and was crucified to take all of our sins away, and that did away with the need for a priest to intercede for us to God.

Once, Jesus Christ died on the cross for our sins, Jesus Christ became the intercessor for man and woman to get to God. The only way you can get your sins forgiven, is go directly to Jesus Christ.

It says this in "The Holy Bible" in first Timothy 2:5, "For there is one God and one Mediator between God and men, the Man Christ Jesus".

In "The Holy Bible", in John 14:6 Jesus says, "I am the way, the truth, and the life. No one comes to the Father, except through Me".

If you have not asked Jesus Christ to take your sins away, and come into your heart, you are a sinner, and you are going to a burning fire hell. It is a real fire that you will burn forever and ever in, and you will never burn up, and you will be forever guilty along with the devil.

You need to confess to Jesus Christ all of your sins, because just like everybody who was ever born, you were born a sinner. And the only way to get to Heaven is to go directly to Jesus Christ, and ask Him to take all of your sins away. If you do not ask Jesus Christ to take all of your sins away, you will go to Hell, and you will not get another chance to go to Heaven.

You do not want to wait, until you die to decide you should have asked Jesus Christ to take your sins away, because no priest can take your sins away. Only Jesus Christ can take your sins away. And if you go to Mother Mary and pray, you are sinning because Mother Mary does not intercede for anybody.

Jesus Christ's mother, Mary, is in Heaven, but she does not help Jesus Christ do what He came to earth to do. Jesus Christ came to earth to take away anybody's sins that will come to Him. And I want Jesus Christ to take all of my sins away, and come into my heart, so when I die, Jesus will take me to Heaven, and I will be with Jesus Christ and everybody who is a Christian.

I beg you to, please, say these words with me, "Jesus Christ, I am a sinner, and I have been a sinner all of my life, and I have cheated and lied, and I do not deserve to get to go to Heaven, but I want to go to Heaven when I die. So Jesus Christ, please, take all of my sins away, because I know that You, Lord Jesus, are the Son of God because that is what it says in the Bible, and I know The Bible is God's Words.

So Jesus Christ, please, I ask You, Lord Jesus, to come into my heart right now, and I am so thankful to You, Jesus Christ, for taking all of my sins away. Thank You, Jesus Christ, for coming into my heart. And now, Jesus Christ, I want to live for You, Lord Jesus, and I want to read "The Holy Bible", and find out what You, Lord Jesus, want to tell me, for myself".

The Ten Commandments are listed in "The Holy Bible", in Exodus 20:1-18:

> I am the Lord thy God.
> Thou shalt have no other gods before me.
> Thou shalt not make unto thee any graven image.
> Thou shalt not take the name of the Lord thy God in vain.
> Remember the Sabbath day to keep it holy.
> Honor thy father and thy mother.
> Thou shalt not kill.
> Thou shalt not commit adultery.
> Thou shalt not steal.
> Thou shalt not bear false witness.

Thou shalt not covet.
And in Mark 12:29-31 in "The Holy Bible" Jesus answered him,
The first of all the commandments is:
Hear, O Israel, the Lord our God;
The Lord is one.
And you shall love the Lord your God with all your heart,
And with all your soul
And with all your mind
And with all your strength
This is the first commandment.

And the second, like it, is this:
You shall love your neighbor as yourself.
There is no other commandment greater than these."

When anybody prays to anyone or anything, or bows down or treats something or anything like a god, they are breaking one of the commandments. It is not acceptable any longer, for people to ask a priest to take their sins away, since, Jesus Christ died on the cross for you and me, and everybody that believes in Him.

In the Old Testament people had to go to a priest, and offer up the perfect and the best animals, in order to have the priest ask God to forgive them for their sins. And then God Sent His Only Son, The Lord Jesus Christ, to the earth to die for all of everybody's sins that believe Jesus Christ is truly the Son of The Living God, who created us in His likeness. So you and everybody that asks Jesus to take away their sins, gets to go to Heaven when they die.

That's where I'm going when I die, I'm going to Heaven, because I asked Jesus Christ to take all of my sins away, and come into my heart. And if you have asked Jesus Christ to take all of your sins away and come into your heart, you will go to Heaven when you die.

Now, what you need to do is live the way Jesus Christ wants you to. And Jesus Christ tells you how to live in "The Holy Bible", and that is the book you need to read, "The Holy Bible".

Jesus Christ died on a cruel, old, rugged cross to shed His Holy Blood for everybody's sins that will believe He is The Son of God. And

He said it was so simple, because you just believe in God, and you believe Jesus Christ is The Son of God, and that Jesus Christ died and shed His Holy Blood, to purify everybody that asks Him to take away their sins, and come into their life.

Wherever you are, even if you are in your car, or even if you are in school, because anywhere at all that you are, anybody can ask Jesus Christ to take away his or her sins, and come into his or her life, and He does right then and there.

You can go directly to Jesus Christ and talk to Him anytime you want to. And Jesus Christ always hears you, and Jesus Christ is always with you, and The Holy Spirit is always with you, once you ask Jesus Christ to take your sins away, and come into your life.

Once you ask Jesus Christ to take away your sins, and come into your heart, you have a desire to know more about Jesus Christ who lives inside you. This same Jesus Christ, who lives inside you, is The Man who loves everybody so much, that He was willing to do what His Father told Him to do.

Jesus' Father told Him to come to earth in the form of a baby, and grow up into The Man who would be crucified for the sins of the world, because it was only through Pure Cleansing Blood, that anybody could be forgiven of his or her sins. Jesus Christ is The Only One who could ever take away any sins, because only God's Son, Jesus Christ, was ever The Perfect Man.

After Jesus Christ takes all of your sins away, and comes into your heart, you feel His Holy Spirit inside you, drawing you to want to talk to Him, and you feel close to God, because Jesus Christ lives inside of you. You talk to Him when you pray, and you can pray without anybody, ever, knowing that you are praying. You can pray in your mind, and you can think prayers to Jesus Christ, and you find yourself not being so afraid, of things that you used to be afraid of.

Once you have asked Jesus Christ to take away your sins, and come into your life, you realize that Jesus Christ has been conquering the enemy for you, when He Conquered the Enemy at Calvary. Do you know where it say in "The Holy Bible", that after you ask Jesus Christ to take away your sins, and come into your heart, that the Holy Spirit is with you always?

It says it right where Jesus Christ tells His disciples that He must go to His Father, in order for The Holy Spirit to come. Jesus Christ then ascended up to Heaven, in the midst of His disciples, and they actually saw Jesus Christ go up to Heaven. Then, on the Day of Pentecost, the Holy Spirit descended in the form of tongues of fire, on the people in the upper room, and they spoke with power from The Holy Spirit, to people of other languages about God and His Son, Jesus Christ.

Another example of The Holy Spirit in "The Holy Bible" is when Jesus Christ was baptized. The Holy Spirit, in the form of a Dove, descended upon Jesus Christ, as soon as Jesus was brought up from the water when He was being baptized.

Conquering the enemy, is the fact, that after you have asked The Lord Jesus Christ to take away your sins, and come into your heart and life, The Lord Jesus Christ conquered the enemy for us, when he gave up his life to save us from our sins, and The Lord Jesus Christ gives you the power of The Holy Spirit.

When The Lord Jesus Christ baptizes you with The Holy Spirit, you are transformed with The Power of The Holy Spirit. It is Power from The Lord Jesus Christ that saves us from our sins, and it is The Power from The Lord Jesus Christ that gives you The Power to live for Christ.

It is The Holy Spirit Power that you get from The Lord Jesus Christ, when He lives in your heart and life. When The Lord Jesus Christ lives within you, your entire being is transformed by The Holy Spirit to want to live for The Lord Jesus Christ. It is The Power of The Holy Spirit that makes you want to do, what Jesus Christ tells you to do in "The Holy Bible".

The Holy Spirit is an inward attitude change that makes you want to tell others about The Lord Jesus Christ. Jesus' Salvation is for everybody that asks Him to take their sins away, and come into their heart and life.

Christ has already conquered the enemy for you for all times, and The Holy Spirit intercedes for you. And when you do not know what to say to The Lord Jesus Christ, The Holy Spirit uses your spirit to talk to Jesus.

There may be times in your life when all you can do is groan inside your heart to God in agony, because some things hurt you so bad that you cannot find words to express how you feel to God, and you cannot express how you feel to anybody.

That is when The Holy Spirit intercedes for you, and lets God know what is going on in your heart and life, and that is when you let The Holy Spirit talk for you to The Lord Jesus Christ, and you, just, let The Holy Spirit intercede in groaning and crying, and praising and thankfulness to The Lord Jesus Christ. That is when you let The Lord Jesus Christ have His way in your heart and life.

It described tongues like fire that sat upon 120 believers in Acts chapter two of "The Holy Bible", and they were all filled with the Holy Ghost, and as the Holy Spirit gave the believers words, they all spoke in other tongues. It was from The Holy Ghost, and it caused people who did not know what the believers were saying, to understand words and to turn to God.

The Holy Spirit came on The Day of Pentecost, in the lives of believers in God, and Jesus Christ, and The Holy Spirit, and the three together is the Trinity.

Speech that may not be interpreted by people, but is from The Holy Ghost, encourages some people to feel the presence of God, also, often it is in times of emotional prayer to God. In which, sometimes, a believer, just, begins to speak words that are given by the Holy Ghost in prayer to God, also, the believer at that time feels The Holy Ghost, literally take over his or her body.

They may feel such closeness with their inner self that gives them, a feeling of power in their spirit. That power from The Holy Ghost, at the same time, causes them to feel extremely humbled and small in the presence of God. It is The Holy Ghost that, also, causes them to feel so loved by God, and so loved by The Lord Jesus Christ.

It says in I Corinthians 14 that Paul instructs people, to pursue the gifts of love and desire spiritual gifts, and that whoever speaks in tongues speaks to God, not to men. It goes on to say, that when you speak in the spirit tongue, you speak mysteries. Furthermore, tongues do not edify other people, for rather somebody prays or sings in tongues, it is edifying oneself. Also, one of the gifts of the spirit is to speak in tongues. For, Paul said when he prayed in tongues his spirit prayed, and he also sang with the spirit.

Paul says in I Corinthians 12:14-15 that he had the gift of tongues, however, it is better to speak five intelligible words, than to speak 10,000 unintelligible words. Paul would pray and sing in tongues with the spirit. However, he would also pray and sing with understanding, that it might draw men to God. He said to desire spiritual gifts of prophesy, so that you may be understood, and so you may by prophesying, edify and exhort and comfort people. Then Paul said in I Corinthians 14:22 that the gifts of tongues are for a sign to unbelievers, and to prophesy is for believers. By the spiritual gift of prophesying, all people learn and are encouraged, and they are drawn to God.

Although, Paul also says in I Corinthians 13:

"Though I speak with the tongues of men and of angels,
But have not love,
I have become sounding brass or a clanging cymbal.
And though I have the gift of prophecy, and understand all mysteries
And all knowledge, and though I have all faith,
So that I could remove mountains,
But have not love,
I am nothing.
And though I bestow all my goods to feed the poor,
And though I give my body to be burned,
But have not love,
It profits me nothing.
Love suffers long and is kind,
Love does not envy,
Love does not parade itself,
Is not puffed up,
Does not behave rudely,
Does not seek its own,
Is not provoked,
Thinks no evil,
Does not rejoice in iniquity,
But rejoices in the truth;
Bears all things,
Believes all things,

Hopes all things,
Endures all things,
Love never fails.
But whether there are prophecies,
They will fail,
Whether there are tongues,
They will cease,
Whether there is knowledge,
It will vanish away.
For we know in part and we prophesy in part,
But when that which is perfect has come,
Then that which is in part will be done away.
When I was a child,
I spoke as a child,
I understood as a child,
I thought as a child,

But when I became a man,
I put away childish things.
For now we see in a mirror, dimly,
But then face to face,
Now I know in part,
But then I shall know just as I also am known.
And now abide faith, hope, love,
These three;
But the greatest of these is love.
I Corinthians 14 instruct us to:
Pursue love,
And desire spiritual gifts,
But especially that you may prophesy.
For he who speaks in a tongue
Does not speak to men
But to God,
For no one understands him;
However, in the spirit he speaks mysteries.
But he who prophesies
Speaks edification and exhortation and comfort to men,

He who speaks in a tongue edifies himself,
But he who prophesies edifies the church.
I wish you all spoke with tongues,
But even more that you prophesied;
For he who prophesies is greater
Than he who speaks with tongues,
Unless indeed he interprets,
So that the church may receive edification…"

I have been in church services where a person spoke a message from The Holy Spirit in tongues. Then another person spoke the message in my language, which is the United States of America English language, and they did not know the situation in my life at that time, however, they spoke directly to me.

Wow! That got scary sometimes, because they were exactly right about a certain fact that just happened in our home, and nobody and I mean nobody, knew about the situation. I had not even made the time to talk to Jesus Christ about it in prayer, but I needed desperate straightening out from God, and I got my help from God without even asking Him for help. I did not tell anybody when messages like that were specifically for me, because I did not want anybody to know I needed a kick in you know what from God.

I get so excited when I read "The Holy Bible", the inspired Words of God, and in John 4:23, Jesus said, "But the hour is coming, and now is, when the true worshipers will worship The Father in spirit and truth, for the Father is seeking such to worship Him. God is Spirit, and those who worship Him must worship in spirit and truth".

Jesus said in John 3:5, "Most assuredly, I say to you, unless one is born of water and the spirit, he cannot enter the kingdom of God. That which is born of the flesh is flesh, and that which is born of the Spirit is spirit. Do not marvel that I said to you, you must be born again. The wind blows where it wishes, and you hear the sound of it, but cannot tell where it comes from and where it goes.   So is everyone who is born of the spirit."

Then in John 3:15, Jesus said, "That whoever believes in Him should not perish but have eternal life", and in John 3:16, Jesus said, "For God so loved the world that He gave His only begotten Son, that whoever believes in Him should not perish but have everlasting life", and in John 3:17, Jesus said, "For God did not send His Son into the world to condemn the world, but that the world through Him might be saved".

Then in John 3:18, Jesus said, "He who believes in Him is not condemned, but he who does not believed is condemned already, because he has not believed in the name of the only begotten Son of God".

In John 8:42, Jesus said, "If God was your Father, you would love me, for I proceeded forth and came from God, nor have I come of myself, but He sent me".

Then in John 14:1, Jesus said, "Let not your heart be troubled; you believe in God, believe also in me".

In John 14:6, Jesus said, "I am the way, the truth, and the life, no one comes to the Father except through me, and no one comes to the Father God our creator, except through Jesus Christ our Lord! Jesus Christ is our Lord and Savior and He is the only way to get to Heaven".

12—It Hurts too Badly

<><><><><><><><><><><><><><><><><><><><><><><><><><><>

When Michael and I lived in Kansas, to help with expenses for our family, I baby sat a lot of children, and I took care of foster care children who lived with us in our church parsonage. Although I applied for small children when we first started out in business taking in foster care children, we got a tiny newborn baby named Gerome, and it was on one of the coldest days of the year in Kansas.

There was sleet and ice on top of several inches of snow when the state women called, and asked if they could bring a newborn baby from the hospital in Lawrence that was probably about twelve miles away from our home. The baby's mother had left the hospital, but the baby was still there. And they needed to find a place for this baby, Gerome, to be cared for, until somebody from the state would come and get him.

Gerome was fun to take care of, and Mike was six years old, and Mary Michelle was three years old, and they both got excited when Gerome came to our home. But they were not prepared for their mommy needing to give almost all of her attention to the new baby. And I was not prepared to take care of a tiny baby that had seizures, because I had never been around anybody that had seizures, and I did not know what to do.

When I needed help I always knew that I could call on any of the many very wonderful friends in our church, and they would come and help my family. We were especially close friends with Maxine and her husband, Virgil, because they were already taking care of a baby placed in their home by the Foster Care Agency. So I got help from them anytime I needed it throughout the years that children were placed in Michael and my home.

Michael was glad that I took care of so many children because all of the checks were in his name, like I had agreed they should be. I never kept any of the money for myself, because my husband paid for our groceries and bills. So, when the state needed someplace to place teenagers, Michael agreed that they could live with us.

A teenage girl, Princess, was placed in our home that was in the church parsonage. I wanted to spoil her, so I got the state to let me purchase new clothes that I said Princess needed. And I took her shopping, while I got Maxine to let me leave Mike and Michelle with her.

Princess liked to watch television, but she always wanted to help me clean up after meals, so I let her because that turned out to be our time to talk and laugh. She had hurtful memories about how unfair life had been for her that she would open up to me about.

I never talked about her memories and I never will, however, I prayed for her, and she felt like a peace had come into her mind. Then I told her that my mom died when I was only eight years old, and my sisters and I would love to have had our mom with us when we were growing up, and maybe, she could try to replace some of her hurtful memories with good thoughts about her mom. Maybe, Princess could consider how hard her mom was working, and trying to make a better life for her children than what she had during her childhood.

Jesus has healed my memories, and I have love in place of hurtful memories from now on. I want healing for my mind and body, so I will not allow any hurtful memories to ruin my health and control how I feel anymore. I am so thankful that Jesus loves everybody, and helps people forget about hurtful stuff.

I am not a slave to hurtful memories. I am only a slave to The Lord Jesus Christ, because that is what I want to be, because Jesus Christ never, ever, hurts anybody. Although, things happen to people, however, Jesus Christ does not cause that, because things happen to everybody, and that is part of life.

Things will happen to me, and my family, and to you if you live long enough. However, do not let those things cause you to have hurtful memories. Just let Jesus Christ take those hurtful memories away. Let your hurtful memories be buried under the blood of our wonderful, Lord Jesus Christ, because after all, Jesus conquered the enemy of hurtful memories at Calvary.

The last children in foster care that we got were Honey who was twelve years old, and Beautiful and she was fourteen years old. They were sisters and they lived with us for probably about two years, and I would like to have adopted both of them, because I have always loved them.

Beautiful and Honey were two of the most precious, pretty children that were placed in our home when we took care of foster care children, and they loved Mike and Michelle. We never forgot them, and oh, how I would love to hold both of those precious, wonderful girls in my arms, and tell them how much I have always loved them, and I have prayed for them a lot of times.

They were both my precious, little girls, and they were especially pretty with their long, brown hair. Beautiful was thin, and Honey was not fat by any means, but she was just a little over-weight because she was still a little girl, but sometimes, she got teased about her weight, and that caused her to have hurtful memories.

So, I talked to her, "Honey, sometimes people say and do terrible, inexcusable things that hurt other people real badly, and I'm so sorry this happened to you".

That is the way it is with God, because God created everything, and that includes the earth, and all the people in it. And God sent his son, Jesus, into the world to teach all of the people about his Father, and how we are supposed to act. Instead of obeying what God told them to do, people disobeyed, and that is sin. So God made it easy for everybody to get the chance to be forgiven, through his son, Jesus, who gave up his life for everybody that will believe in him, and confess their sins to him, and ask Jesus to come into their hearts and life.

Well, some things happened that caused me to cry so much that I thought our marriage was over, and it hurts too badly to ever talk about any of it, and I want to be at peace.

However, I am writing about my rings because a miracle happened for me.

I was standing in front of our church door that was at the top of several steps, and I turned around and started crying, hysterically. Then

I struggled to get my wedding rings off, and then I held them up over the top of my head, and threw them as far as I could, because I thought our marriage was over.

However, Jesus saw my tears and heard my painful cry, and helped me, and our marriage survived.

13—Dreams and Angels

We all looked for my rings, but we could never find them, so we gave up trying, and Michael said my rings were lost for good. So he bought me a new set of rings for Christmas that year, and he tried to treat me better.

We lived in our church parsonage, and Michael was concerned that when we got old, and when we retired we would not have a home to live in. So since there was a real estate agent, Collene, in our church, we talked to her about how we could get a home without any down payment.

So after I took Mike to school one day, I drove around the neighborhood that was close to the grade school. And there was a real estate sign in front of a yellow house, so I stopped to look at it, since there was somebody inside. Then after talking with the real estate lady that was there, she showed my little girl, Michelle, and I the house that my husband and I ended up buying.

This home was very nice and completely fixed up before we moved into it, because some people in our church, Virgil and Calvin, helped us fix it up before we moved out of the parsonage, also my dad, Larry, often helped Michael work on this home. Then people from our church had a nice house warming party for us after we moved into our new and first home.

I worked at the bank in Eudora, for one school year. And during that time, I still prayed and read God's Word, and sang to Jesus when I played my piano, as much as could. And I had several dreams that the wedding rings that I had thrown in my anguish, were in front of me. I would dream that there was a little boy with dark hair standing in front of me, and he was handing me my wedding rings.

The dreams got to be so frequent that I would toss and turn, and wake up. Sometimes, I would wake up with a start, because they seemed so real. Then Michael got me beautiful, new rings as a Christmas gift, after I was without rings for several months. Now, here it was almost three years later, and the rings had never been found, and we had given up on ever finding them.

When I was working late on a Friday evening in the bank, somebody told me that I had a phone call. There was a lady, Mary, who attended our Assembly of God Church, as often as her family could, and she told me that her little boy, Jeff, had been playing close to the church, where there was a place for water to empty into a sewer.

Jeff used to be in children's church, when I taught that at our church, so I knew him well. Anyway, his mother told me that Jeff found some wedding rings. She asked me if I ever found my rings that were lost, almost three years earlier.

I was totally surprised, because nobody had found my rings. Although, several times, during that three years Michael and friends of ours looked for them. We told people that I lost my rings, but we never let anybody know, why I lost them.

However, God knows all, and He blesses His children anytime He wants to. And I truly thank The Lord Jesus Christ for all of His many blessings.

Within ten minutes after Mary called me, she brought Jeff to the bank.

I was busy working, when somebody said, "Hey, there's a kid here that wants to see you".

I looked up from my work, and it was, just exactly, like in all of the dreams that I had been having for several weeks.

I saw the little boy with dark hair that had always been in my dreams. He held out his hand, and my wedding rings were in the palm of his hand.

Some people do not believe that God gives people dreams. Well, I sure do, *and, I know, that I know,* those dreams were from our Lord and Savior, our Almighty God.

14—The Fear of Homelessness

<><><><><><><><><><><><><><><><><><><><><><><><><><><><>

Michael told me, shortly after we moved to Danville, that he was too sick to work long enough that he could provide for us. So it all depended on me from then on if we lost everything that we had worked for in our marriage. And if I did not get a job that could provide for our family, we would lose everything we had.

We would lose our children, because they would have to live with relatives, or whoever could take care of them. And we would be homeless, if we lost our possessions, so I needed to get a job and fast.

The only thing, I knew how to do that I could make decent money at, was to baby-sit and be a homemaker. I had three children at home, and Michael depended on me to take care of him when he was too sick to take care of himself.

I had a baby-sitting license like I had when we lived in Kansas. But I had to give it up shortly after I got it, because people in Kansas told the state licensing board that my husband was abusive to me. And the Illinois licensing board did not allow me to live with Michael and baby-sit both.

Michael had become the preacher in the family, and he was perfect in the eyes of his parents and sister, and that's the way I wanted it to be, too. I wanted everybody to always see my husband that I loved so much, as a perfect man, and husband to me, and father to our children. And I still, to this very day, want everybody to know that my husband was perfect, because my husband was no worse than anybody else ever was, because we can look at some of the men in the Bible.

Some men, highly esteemed by God, did some very bad things. Just look at King Saul in The Old New Testament. He was anointed king by the prophet of God, and he was so jealous of David that he tried to have David killed.

Peter was one of Jesus most loved friends, but he denied Jesus three times when Jesus needed him the most, and Jesus forgave Peter.

And Jesus forgave my husband for anything and everything that he ever did, and Jesus forgave me for all of my sins.

And if you have asked Jesus to take all of your sins away, and to come into your heart and life, Jesus has forgiven you, and that makes you a forgiven sinner, and your sins are gone.

I did not know God was so in control of my life that my baby-sitting days were over. I thought I gave up my license to baby-sit, because I chose my husband over my job.

However, I soon came to realize that God was going to give me another ministry that would be a lot harder, and more demanding that I was not prepared for. And if I had known in advance, that it was going to take such hard work, I would never have done what I did.

Michael told me that we were going to be homeless because neither one of us had a job. We would lose everything, because there was no way to pay for our house.

I would be homeless, but he always had a home, because he could live with his mom and dad. And they would probably let Rachelle stay with them, as long as he lived with them. But he did not know where I would live, or where Michelle and Mike would live.

I got paid to take care of Michael's elderly aunt, Aunt Lucille, so she was staying with us. And we used the money to pay for almost all of the utilities, and put some on our house payments. However, we were going to be homeless, if I did not make more money than that.

So bright and early the next morning, Michael told me that I had to take Aunt Lucille with me and apply for jobs. He even went out applying for any job that he could get, and he would have been a cab driver, or a newspaper boy, or anything that gave him money to provide for his family.

Then that night over dinner we would compare notes on what we had applied for, and hopefully got. I needed to be back at home before 3:30, so I could have dinner on the table at 5:00 because we always ate at 5:00; since that was the time his parents always ate. And dinner was always a big meal, and we all sat down at the table, and ate together as a family.

Aunt Lucille went with me, while I was applying for jobs, but nobody would hire me. I went to the hospital and filled out an application, and wrote that I would work in the kitchen, or even clean toilets, or mop floors, or anything, if they would, please, give me a job

My family would be homeless; very soon, if I did not get a job. But I was told that they had younger people with experience that could do those jobs.

I was discouraged, however, I just kept right on looking for any job that I could get.

I waited in line at the unemployment offices, and they told me to go to the community college, and get tested to see what I could qualify for. So I went there, and I was tested and told by a counselor that I was not qualified to do anything.

The counselor told me the only thing I could do was baby-sit, or be a nanny and live with people. He also told me that I was too old because I was forty, and nobody hires people without experience that are forty or older.

I left the job center at the community college with tears in my eyes. And Aunt Lucille was with me, and she needed to use a restroom. So, we went inside a big building, to use the restroom

Then a woman saw me, and recognized me from when I was a teenager in some of her classes in high school. And she told me that was her last day to work at this college, because she was retiring and the semester was over.

She explained to me that she lost contact with me after my family moved from Rankin, Illinois. Then we talked for awhile, and I told her that if I did not find a job real soon, my family would lose everything we had, and we would be homeless, so she had an idea.

Then she asked me, if I had my life to start all over again, what would I do?

I replied, "That's not possible, I'm going to be forty years old in about six weeks, and nobody can start their life over, and I love having my husband and children".

Then she insisted, if you had a chance to be anything that you want to be, besides being married and having your children, what would you be?

I wanted to leave because I needed to apply for jobs, so I quickly mumbled, "A nurse, I'd be the best nurse that I could possibly be".

So she told me, you can be a nurse then, and this is Friday and classes start up Monday morning, so I'll get you right into classes, if you're ready to start.

I was anxious, and I replied, I don't have time to go to school. I need to get a job real fast or my family will be homeless. We only have $540.00 to our name, and that is from when I baby-sat.

She insisted that was exactly how much I needed to pay for the first class. And she went on to say that I wanted to be a nurse, and that was what I was going to be. And I needed to write a check, and she would get me enrolled.

Well, dummy me!

I obeyed anybody that told me what to do, because I had been taught all of my life to do what I was told. I was afraid of people who were in control of me because many times I got punished just for looking like I was not happy.

So, I obeyed that teacher, and I wrote the check.

She said, your first class is rhetoric and it is on computers, and you can do it. I know you can do it, because of all the things in your life that you have over-come.

You are a real hard worker, and you would not be here today sitting in that chair if you had given up. All you have to do is show up for classes, and work at learning as hard as you have your whole life through. But you will need to take extra classes, to prepare yourself for the classes that need to be taken, in order to prepare you to be a nurse.

With that, I was getting anxious because I did not have time to full around with school or anything.

I asked, "How long will that take me, because I need a job right now? It looks like there are a lot of classes written on that paper, and I don't have time for anything extra. If it is God's will for me to be a nurse, God will help me do what I have to do, and forget about anything extra".

Then she encouraged me, you have your work cut out for you, however, if you think you can do it, you can, so we'll go right for the top. I will not sign you up for any classes, except the ones you have to take to be a nurse. If you find out you need more classes to help you with any of the classes I sign you up for, you can always take them, and then continue with the ones I am signing you up for, but just don't tell anyone you can't do it. Since you have succeeded this far in life, and you have a great faith in God, I'm sure you can do it.

I had great faith in this home-economics teacher, who I had at Rankin High School. Although I needed a job right then, she encouraged me to be the nurse that I wanted to be, and I knew I could make money at that. There was always a need for nurses, and I thought that was good because I would always have a job.

I thought it was a weird thing that I had our check book with me that day, because I did not know I was going to be using it. So I wrote a check to Danville Area Community College for $540.00 and handed it to her. Then she gave me a paper that listed the classes that I needed to take to become a nurse.

Then she hugged me and said she was retiring, and that day was her last day to work at that college, and she had faith in me. And we both wondered about us coming together on her last day in that college, but we knew that was God.

God is, so, totally, in control of my life, and God knew that would happen, and whatever God has for me, I want. Thank You, Lord Jesus, because it was God that had me sign up, and give our last penny to be in the center of God's will for my life, and the lives of our family. Oh, I just thank you so very much, God, for all of Your Goodness. You are so Majestic, Lord God, and I can't thank You enough for Your Goodness, Lord Jesus.

I was very happy and got home and fixed an especially nice dinner. And I had our meal on the table when my family sat down to eat. Then after Michael blessed the meal, he told us all about his day, and then our children talked. Aunt Lucille and I listened quietly, as usually, and after that, I asked if I could make an announcement.

I announced with great enthusiasm, "Monday morning I am going to start going to college, and I am going to be a nurse".

Michael demanded a good explanation from me about why I did not get a job, instead of thinking that I could possibly be smart enough to go to college, because I was crazy, and I boarder-lined on a mental case. And where did I plan on getting the money to pay for college.

I quietly answered my husband, "I've already paid for my summer class, and I will start Monday morning. There was $540.00 left from when I baby-sat, and I used it to pay for my summer class. By going to college, I'll get to become a nurse, and we will use all of the money to pay bills for living expenses".

My husband was not happy with me to say the least, because he was sure that I had just wasted the last dollar to our name.

And I thought my husband was right, because when it came right down to it, his parents would always be there for him.

Michael called some friends of ours, and told them about the "foolish" thing I had done that day, so they came over to our home. And one of our friends cornered me, and told me that I should be ashamed of myself for only thinking about myself when I signed up for college.

She told me that I wasted the last penny that I had left from baby-sitting. Where did I think I would ever come up with any other money to pay for books and other classes? I could be sure that none of her family would ever help me.

Michael was sick, and I needed to take care of him and his aunt. And Rachelle needed to have her mother around all of the time. And who did I think I was, and did I really think I was smart enough to go to college?

Who did I think I was to use the last dollar that was from my baby-sitting days?

Mary Michelle was truly proud that her mommy was going to start going to college on Monday morning. So, she called up her best friend that was her cousin, Joni, and she was, also, very proud that I was going to college.

My daughter and Joni was what I needed to help me feel good about my decision to go to college. So I made up my mind, right then and there, that I would give it my very best.

I would study as hard as I could. If I failed a class I would take it all over, again and again, until, I passed it so I could go on to another class.

Abused, Conquered, Alive!!!

I asked God to help me. If it was truly God's will, like I thought it was, for me to go to college and be a nurse, God would help me.

Michael's parents took Aunt Lucille home with them, because they said I could not take her to college classes with me. Then Michael told me the best advice he could give to me was to take notes, and write down everything the instructors wrote on the blackboards. And I should ask as many questions as I needed to, if I did not completely understand what the instructors said.

The next day was Saturday, and Mary Michelle went to work at Sears. She proudly told her friends that her mommy was going out to Danville Area Community College to get books, because her mommy was going to be a nurse. Rachelle got up early on Saturdays and watched cartoons, so she was already up and asked if she could go with me. So I fixed her hair and kissed her daddy good-bye, and off Rachelle and I went to the college.

Michael asked me where I thought I would get the money to buy books, and I answer my husband that I did not know where the money could come from. If I was truly in the center of God's will, like I thought I was, so then it was up to God. I just knew that I was on my way to the bookstore in the college to get books; so I could start going to college on Monday.

When Rachelle and I got to the college bookstore, I went up to the desk where a woman was taking money from people who were buying books. I told her that I was going to start going to college on Monday morning, and I did not have any money to pay for books.

Well, she studied my schedule of classes for that summer. Then she handed me all of the books, pens and pencils, and a brand new book bag that she put all of the stuff inside. She also put highlighters and several tablets into the book bag. And I just kept watching her, without saying a word.

Rachelle, my little, darling, baby girl had just turned eight years old, and she saw all of the stuff that the clerk was putting into the book bag for me. So, of course, she saw everything that her mommy was getting, and she knew I always got stuff for her. So Rachelle was looking at some pretty pencils and notebooks and candy.

Well, the lady took that stuff from her, and put it into a bag and handed it to her. And then the clerk asked me, "Is there anything else I can get for you or your daughter?"

I told the clerk, "I don't have any money, at all, and the only thing I have to, actually, have is a book, so I can go to this college and become a nurse".

She pointed to a tall man with white hair, who was standing to one side of the bookstore, and I glanced at him, and he smiled.

And the clerk told me, "That's the Dean of this college, and he had already given me the okay to give you everything you wanted".

"They must want you at this college, girl, because they do that for every so many people who are in real need of books and stuff."

After Rachelle and I got home later that Saturday morning, Michael was very upset to say the least, when we came into our home with all that new stuff, and he wanted to know how I paid for all of it.

I felt so intimidated by then that I could hardly speak, as I quietly told my husband that the college gave me the stuff.

With that, Michael called the college bookstore, and talked with the clerk that confirmed what I said was right.

She let Michael know that it was something the college did from time to time for people who seemed like they would make it in college, if they got the chance, and they could not come up with any money to pay for it. And even if I did not make it through college, I would not have to pay it back. Because the college was using it as an incentive to hope I would stay in college, and make something of myself.

That was just what they saw in me, when the teacher that I had in high school gave the Dean of the college the information on me the day before, when she enrolled me in that college. Because she told me to come to the college bookstore in the morning, which I did, and this Dean of the college wanted to see me. And he agreed that I seemed like somebody that might make it in the college.

On Monday morning, I kissed my babies, Rachelle, Mary Michelle, and Mike, and we all went off in different directions. Rachelle went to Liberty Grade School, and it was real good that she was finally comfortable in school again, because she did not want to move from our comfort zone to another town and school. And I did not want to move either, however, we moved and we were here to stay.

For the first few weeks, after we moved to this new home, Rachelle would cling to me and cry, and beg me not to leave her at that school where everything was strange to her. The classrooms were completely different from anything we had ever seen, because all of them were open. And everybody could be seen in other areas of the room, where they gathered around their teachers for the grades they were in. But the worst part about Rachelle's new school was that she did not know anybody there.

My little Baby Rachelle's daddy was in the hospital in Kansas City from having cancer surgery, and she was very worried about him. Her brother, Mike, was finishing up a semester at college in Kansas, so I was doing all of the business things that needed to be done after a person moves; like address changes, and license plates, and unpacking and cleaning. And then I could get my license to do the baby-sitting business in our home, like I had in Kansas, for so many years.

Our son, Mike, went to Danville Area Community College to get an associate's degree in law, and in 1992 he graduated. We were all so very proud of our Mike, because if anybody was ever going to make it in life, Mike was. He was a real hard worker and he was very committed.

Mike always helped his dad and me around the house, plus, he worked at jobs and paid for his own car, and his own college education. He gave money to Michael that helped us buy groceries and gas for the cars, and he always got involved in things at church, and I especially liked it, because Mike had very good manners.

Mary Michelle was still in high school, and she always made such good grades that she was going to graduate early. She had worked at jobs ever since she was fourteen-years old, and bought her own clothes and things for school, and that included her own car. Mary also bought things for her little sister, Rachelle, and she helped take care of her, like her brother did.

Well, now that I was in college, I would sit in a seat in front of the teacher's desk, because I did not want to miss a thing, and I wanted the teachers to always see that I was not cheating. Because students did not write their names on their papers and tests that they handed in; they wrote their social security numbers on the papers. And I could never remember my number, so I would look at my social security card and write the numbers down.

Before I took Chemistry, I said to the instructor, "Please, just let me audit this class, and then I can take it again with a grade. I know it is not a subject that I know anything about, and I will not pass it. Also, I have such a full schedule already for this summer, that there's no way I can give it the study time that I will need for it".

The chemistry instructor told me to stand up, so the class could see me when he talked about me, and what he said was truly kind. Mary wants to audit this chemistry class for this summer, and I know she can pass it, because she is smart and she studies a lot. How many of you students think she will pass this class, if she takes it for a grade?

Every student in that chemistry class raised their hand. And many of them said they had me in other classes that they were in, and I could do it. So, as scared as I was, I agreed to take the class for a grade.

Well, when it came time for the final in that class and the tests were handed out, my mind went so blank that the entire test looked foreign to me. And I was still trying to figure out how to answer the first question, when the instructor said time was almost up. So I took my test papers to this instructor and told him that I had drawn a blank, and I could not even answer the first question.

Then the instructor stood up at his desk and told the class that he wanted their attention for just a minute. I was about to pass out, and I was just sick to my stomach with so much stress. I knew it was too late for me to do the test, so I would have to take a failing grade for this chemistry class.

However, God was in control of my life, and I was not in control of anything. And God wanted to show me how much He was with me.

This chemistry instructor informed the class that I had drawn a blank; I was not able to even answer one question on the final exam. He knew that I could answer every question on that exam, and he wanted to see a show of hands from everyone that agreed with him.

I was so stressed out and scared that I could not tell if everybody raised their hands, although, the chemistry instructor said it was unanimous. So he had another class teacher escort me to a quieter room that was enclosed with windows, and I took the final exam.

Man, that exam was hard! However, it was no harder than any of the other final exams that I had to take after each class was completed. And, I got an A for class.

I took notes on everything the instructors said, and I asked them to, please, repeat things that I did not understand. Also, I wrote down and copied everything the instructors put on the black boards. And of course, I read and studied the material in all of the books that we were told to read. And I made friends with a real lot of the other students in the classes, and that I heard had already taken the classes.

Well, I made as many friends in classes as I could, and studied with everybody that wanted to study together. Some of them had already taken classes that I was in, and they let me borrow their notes. Then I shared my notes with students who could not come to all of the classes, and that gave me the golden opportunity to let Christ's love shine through me. And, of course, I was careful not to miss classes.

The most important thing I did was pray, and ask God to always help me, and give God the praise and glory due Him for every paper and project and test that I did. And this caught onto other students that worked on projects and studied with me. It was so great, because several men and women that studied with me asked God for help, too.

That went on for the entire four years, including summers that I was in college. And I let God shine, so miraculously, through my life that it drew others to ask me how I did it, and then I got to tell them God did it through me.

I was not surprised at how many people became my friends when I was in college, but what I did not know was that God was going to use me in college to help draw people to Jesus.

My own husband, Michael, saw how God was blessing me in college, and he prayed the sinner's prayer along with me, and he became a real sweetheart, and apologized for being mean to me. However, he was so used to being mean that it was hard for him not to remain that way. So he would get mean, but of course, I never held it against him, and he would ask God to forgive him all over again.

The first test in college that I took, Michael asked me what my grade was, and I was embarrassed to admit to him, that I did so badly that the instructor did not even bother to grade it. I thought that she just gave me 10 points for doing it. Then almost every test after that I got the same thing on it.

I was in a class called Rhetoric I that was all done on computers, which was the first time I ever sat in front of a computer.

One of my instructors for Physical Science was Dr. Merrill O'Brien, and he needed somebody to help him show the class how to do complicated equations on the board and chemistry lab work. Then Dr. O'Brien always let me be the student who showed the other students how to figure it all out.

So Dr. O'Brien let me help him every day. He would tell the class that he was amazed at how much I knew about all of the material that was presented in his class, and other classes that he heard that I was in from other instructors, so he said I would make a good college instructor.

When I was in Rhetoric II it was all done on computers, too. And I was told that I needed to take classes that would prepare me for that class, and I needed to learn how to write papers.

Well, when I handed in my draft, like we were supposed to and it was graded, I did not have a chance of passing that class. So I knew college had come to an end for me, unless God came through.

I did not have time to take extra classes, and put my nursing classes on hold. My husband was having more cancer surgeries, and I had to get a job to take care of our family. We would be homeless, if I did not get a job.

When I applied at the hospital my application was not even considered, because I was forty years old. I did not have any experience, to, so much as, work as a cook, or a cleaning lady, or dishwasher or any kind of a job, not even part time, or at all. No place in or around Danville would hire me, because I did not have any experience; which was what they all told me, when I applied for a job.

We were going to be homeless! Michael could just see it coming!

Michael could not work very much because he was sick. Although, he mowed and cleaned the neighbors' yards, and I cleaned the neighbor's house, and that included washing all of the walls, ceilings and windows. I got $80.00 for that, but they said it was more than they could afford.

I was real discouraged after I left Rhetoric II, because I realized that before I could continue to go to college to be a nurse, I would need to take a lot of other classes, and then retake Rhetoric II.

So, I was down on my knees next to our bed praying and crying my heart out to God, when my husband came home from cleaning the neighbor's yard.

I was so sick at heart that I ached all over, because I knew Michael was right, when he said I would never make it in college, because I was too dumb. And how could I have ever thought that I could possibly go to college.

Michael said, sooner or later, I would get into a class that was way over my head, and I would be done with going to college.

And he was so right, and I was so dumb. And I could not feel the presence of God, at all. Where was God when I needed Him now?

Now, the time had come that not even Michael could help me write a research paper. And I did not know how to begin to write something like a research paper.

Mike said he could not understand what the instructor wanted, when he tried to read the instructions that told what was expected in the research paper. Instructions had changed so much since Mary Michelle had written research papers in high school, that she knew there was no way she could really help me.

I prayed and cried so hard, and I did not feel like God was around any place.

Then I gave up and prayed to God, "Lord, if it is Your Will for me to be a nurse, I have to go to college and learn how to be one, in order to get a job and support my family. If it is not Your Will for me to be a nurse and support my family, let me get another job, I pray in Jesus Name, Amen".

Well, as soon as I said, "Amen", a woman's name came into my mind, and the woman's name was Norma. *And, I knew, that I knew,* that Norma was going to help me with my research paper.

Because God was going to use me as a helper in time of need to Norma, and her need was that she had been an English teacher, and she was in need of encouragement from God. I was so busy going to college and studying, and all about myself, but I needed to let God use me to be a helper.

I called Norma, and she was glad to help me with my research paper.

God truly was in control of my family and me. And Norma and I became very good friends.

I did not know that my instructor had just been diagnosed with melanoma cancer, when I wrote my research paper entitled "My Husband's Battle with Melanoma Cancer".

Then I talked all about it in front of the class. Because I knew so much about it from living with Michael, the speech went perfect. Also, I answered all of the questions from the guests and faculty, and the students that were in the classroom.

My family was going to be homeless, if I did not make it in college, so I could get a job. So I would work as hard as I had to, in order to keep us from being homeless.

I got paid for baby-sitting in the church nursery, so that was a help to our family. And Michael would get a job around Danville for a few days or weeks, and that was great. However, because he was sick with melanoma cancer, he would have to quit.

We never had enough money to pay the doctor and hospital bills that kept right on coming in the mail, and we did not have insurance to pay the hospital or doctors. It truly looked like we were going to have to let our home go back to the bank, because taxes and insurance on it and the cars were coming due. And there was not a penny left to pay for them, after we bought what groceries and gas we had to have, in order to survive.

I could not take care of my husband's Aunt Lucille very often, because I was taking a real full load of classes in school, so I studied all of the time. Although we got money for letting her stay with us, that I used to help pay for the house payments. However, now the house payments were turning into bigger and bigger unpaid bills.

15—POVERTY

◇◇◇◇◇◇◇◇◇◇◇◇◇◇◇◇◇◇◇◇◇◇◇◇◇◇◇◇◇◇◇◇◇◇◇◇◇◇

Where would I ever come up with the money to pay for myself to get to attend college?

I signed up for anything that was free, because we were always in the poverty range when I filled out papers, and we got the most commodities that were given out to poor families. We were poor according to what the government listed, as, how much money a family needed, in order to survive.

That is the way it always was during my marriage to my husband, Michael Proctor. And I waited in many lines throughout our marriage to get anything that we could to help our family eat, and get the medical needs that were so appreciated from our government.

I thank God that we live in this Wonderful United States of America, where we can get food and supplies and medical needs met, if we just put forth the effort that it takes to apply for things, and to show up and stand in line and wait for them.

My family and I live in this great United States of America, and I pray that God is always with our wonderful country. I pray for God's protection and help so that we do not lose our freedom, and I pray for our country to seek God.

There were some ways to help get college paid for, and that was to apply for scholarships. Then wait until committees in charge of each scholarship determined who got each one, and that is just what I did.

I filled out every scholarship that I could, and each one took time because there were questions on them, which I focused on just like the questions on all of the tests that I took in college. I always prayed over the scholarship papers that I filled out before I turned them in, just like I prayed over the tests that I took in college.

After I finished my first class at Danville Area Community College, Michael told me somebody from the college called when I was gone, and wanted me to return their call. It turned out that the college wanted me to come and answer some questions, and I needed to come to a theater room where there was enough room for everybody to sit.

I could have my husband come with me, and they would like to meet him. But Michael refused to be any part of me and the college, because I studied so much, and he thought I had done something wrong.

He would say, "You aren't going to make it in college, because nobody studies like you do, Mary, it shows how dumb you are, because nobody has to study that much when they are in school!"

Of course, that always hurt when Michael made fun of me, because one of my biggest weaknesses in my life was that I hated to be made fun of. So I would break down and cry, although, I always pulled myself together, as quickly as I could, because there was no time for tears and crying.

I had to keep on studying, because I did not want my family to become homeless. If I did not make it in college and get a job, that's exactly what was going to happen to us. We would end up losing everything we had, and we would be homeless!

Although my husband worked at any job he could get, even when he had melanoma cancer inside his organs, it was never enough money to pay the house payments. Then I had used the last of my baby-sitting money to pay for myself to start going to college, and that was $540.00.

Now, we did not have any more money, at all.

We never told our children that we were going to be homeless, because we tried to always keep things like that from them. We wanted to protect our children, and we did not want them to worry about our finances.

I thought the faculty was going to tell me, because I did not have any more money to pay for myself to continue to take any more classes, they were going to dismiss me from this college.

As Mary Michelle and I sat in the theater room at the college, I was praying in my thought life, as I often did. Then when a member of the staff got up in front of the audience to talk, I glanced at my daughter.

I could see an Angel sitting there so close to my daughter that they could have been one person!

Mary Michelle had a glow all over her body that caused her to, just shine, and her big, beautiful, blue eyes sparkled.

I could not take my eyes off this Angel and Mary Michelle!

As I stared in amazement at this Angel and my daughter, I wondered if I was, actually, imagining that I saw this Angel. Because I was under a lot stress, what with going to college and studying so hard, all the time. Then, of course, I had the presence of The Lord with me all the time.

I had been studying and thinking about how Angels are with us, so maybe, I was seeing what was in my imagination.

I asked Jesus to, please, help me study and see what I needed to learn before I took tests. So I would focus on everything instructors told us and wrote on the blackboards. Then, of course, I would study, over and over, everything that I wrote down; which instructors would write on the blackboards, and in homework that they gave to students.

I would study a lot, and then I would look away, and I would picture what I was concentrating on. And I would see in my mind things that instructors wanted students to learn.

Then I would make myself concentrate, and see in front of my eyes what I needed to remember. And, of course, nobody else could see those things. It was me that was making my mind see things that instructors were teaching us.

It was what I had done many times throughout my life, as a coping mechanism, when there was too much stress in my life for me to deal with.

I would focus on something so much that I would see it, as though, it was really part of what was going on in the true life. Although, sometimes, I sensed that I had to make myself dismiss what I was seeing, to also keep from losing my mind. I did not want to confuse reality with my imagination, in that almost everybody has an imagination.

It is a fact that people have to make sure they do not go crazy by letting their imaginations take over what is true and real. If it is truly something that is actually a real thing that can be touched or felt, other people can see it, too.

And, of course, it will not disappear in front of you, unless, somebody takes it away, or there is a big storm that blows it away, or the ground gives way, and causes it to fall or something causes it to blow up, or catch on fire. I never wanted to confuse my imagination with reality

However, I had seen something. I felt so much peace in my heart, and I sensed that the presence of The Holy Spirit was with my daughter, Mary Michelle, and me at that very moment.

I felt such love and thankfulness for my precious daughter, and that The Lord Jesus helped me raise her for Him. I sensed that Jesus knew all about Mary Michelle and me. I knew that Jesus knows all about everything, *and, I knew that I knew,* that the Thing That Matters Is That We Are On Our Way to Heaven!

Then I started quietly thanking Jesus in my thoughts and mind, because of what happened right after that.

The speaker in that theater was calling my name, and she was telling the audience about me.

I was called to come to the front and get a scholarship. And I got a check for $540.00, and I was told that it was for me to take home! Praise God! Thank You, Jesus!

Then, from time to time throughout the following years, I got different chances to apply for scholarships. They were the same applications for scholarships that committees gave to any student who wanted to take advantage of opportunities.

Then all students needed to do, was to apply for the scholarships, and fill them out exactly like the questions asked. Then they needed show up at the scholarship committee meetings, when they were called to come and meet the members of the scholarship team.

Almost every scholarship that I applied for was given to me. My college bills were all paid, and anything to do with going to college was paid by different scholarship committees.

That was all a gift from God!

I said a short speech in appreciation to all of the people for their goodness to me. And I thanked all of the people throughout my years, while I was going to college to be a Bachelor of Science Registered Nurse.

Michael was very happy about the scholarship that I had gotten, and I gave him the check for $540.00.

You cannot out give God! You, just, can never, ever, out give God! God is so very, tremendously wonderful, and nobody can ever out give God! God will give it all right back to you! And He will give you way over in abundance, of what your wildest imaginations can ever think of!

Jesus Christ was crucified to forgive anybody of their sins that asks Him to, and to come into their life, and then, Jesus Christ arose from the grave, and appeared to his eleven disciples that had not betrayed Him.

In Mark 16:14, Jesus Christ rebuked them, for not believing those who He had appeared to before them, and Jesus Christ said to them, "Go into all, the world and preach the gospel to every creature, he who believes and is baptized will be saved, but he who does not believe will be condemned, and these signs will follow those who believe:

In My name they will cast out demons;   and they will speak with new tongues; they will take up serpents, and if they drink anything deadly, it will by no means hurt them, they will lay hands on the sick, and they will recover", and when Jesus Christ finished saying these words, in Mark 16:18, He was lifted up into Heaven, and The Holy Ghost came to be with people.

When I was only three years old, I knew that I was a sinner, because when my mom asked me if I wanted to have Jesus take my sins away and come into my heart, I knew in my simple little mind, that I had never asked Jesus to take my sins away, and I also knew that Jesus did not live in my heart.

The Holy Ghost was using my mom to help me come to Jesus, and I asked Jesus, for myself, to take my sins away, and come into my heart! After I accepted The Lord Jesus Christ into my heart, I was totally aware of Jesus presence with me for the rest of my life. It was the Holy Spirit in my heart, and life that Jesus said would come to be with people, after He was taken up into Heaven.

The Holy Spirit is the third part of the Trinity, because there is God the Father, Jesus Christ God's Son, and the Holy Spirit, which make up the Trinity, and they all three exist together as one God, but yet, they all three exist separately. The Lord Jesus Christ is God's Son, and He depends on His Father, and The Holy Spirit depends on both God the Father and the Lord Jesus Christ, so this is the order that the Trinity is made of.

The fact that Jesus Christ does the will of His Father is found in Philippians 2:6, "Who being in the form of God, did not consider it robbery to be equal with God, but made Himself of no reputation, taking the form of a bondservant.

And coming in the likeness of men, and being found in appearance as a man, He humbled Himself and became obedient to the point of death, even, the death of the cross. Therefore God also has highly exalted Him and given Him the name, which is above every name, that at the name of Jesus every knee should bow, of those in Heaven, And of those on earth, and of those under the earth, and that every tongue should confess that Jesus Christ is Lord, to the glory of God the Father"!

The ministry that the Holy Spirit does, with the help of both God the Father and the Lord Jesus Christ, is found in John 16:13. Jesus said, "However, when He, the Spirit of truth, has come, He will guide you into all truth. For He will not speak on His own authority, but whatever He hears He will speak, and He will tell you things to come. He will glorify me for He will take of what is mine, and declare it to you. All things that the Father has are mine, therefore I said that He will take of mine, and declare it to you. A little while, and you will not see me, and again a little while, and you will see me, because I go to the Father".

The Trinity working together is found in second Corinthians 13:14, which says, "The grace of the Lord Jesus Christ, and the love of God, and the communion of the Holy Spirit be with you all". The Trinity is found in baptism in water in Matthew 28:18, where it says, "All authority has been given to me in Heaven and on earth. Go therefore and make disciples of all the nations, Baptizing them in the name of The Father, and of the Son, and of the Holy Spirit, teaching them to observe all things that I have commanded you, I am with you always, even to the end of the age".

Most of my life, I have been taught that The Holy Spirit of God the Father, and Christ Jesus our Lord and Savior is dwelling within God's people. There is a Holy presence that you may feel, once Christ Jesus has come into your heart and life.

However, for the first fifty years of my life, I was taught that you get The Holy Spirit when you speak in tongues. And that is a language known only to God, because it is a Heavenly language. I was taught that you did not have The Holy Spirit, unless you spoke in tongues. I was also taught that you could lose The Holy Spirit easily, if you did not speak in tongues regularly.

I will not tell people that they are going to Hell Fire and Brimstone because they do not pray like I do. People need to read "The Holy Bible", and find out for themselves how to pray.

Jesus gave people an example of how to pray, according to The Lord's Prayer, in Matthew 6:9.

> Our Father in heaven,
> Hallowed be
> Your name
> Your kingdom come,
> Your will be done.
> On earth as it is in Heaven.
> Give us this day our daily bread.
> And forgive us our debts,
> As we forgive our debtors.
> And do not lead us into temptation,
> But deliver us from the evil one. For
> Yours is the kingdom and the power
> And the glory forever…
> Amen.

All through my life, I was drawn by the Holy Spirit to read "The Holy Bible". The Holy Spirit, also, used other people throughout my life to encourage me to read, and study "The Holy Bible" for myself.

As a simple little child, I studied and still study "The Holy Bible", because I believe it is the inspired Words of God, written by God's chosen people. Then after I got married to Michael, and we went into the ministry, I taught a club for girls, Missionettes, and they got to learn the same beliefs that I have.

In the *"Missionettes Handbook"* that The Assemblies of God District has printed, it even listed what they believe, and this is what I have believed my entire life through.

I believe in the whole Word of God, and I believe that God is God, and God has always been God, and that God will always be God of Heaven and of earth, and everything in between Heaven and earth, and I believe that Jesus Christ is God's only begotten Son, Our Savior.

I believe that God sent His only begotten Son, The Lord Jesus Christ, into the world to save the lost, and broken hearted from their sins, and that it is only through asking The Lord Jesus Christ for forgiveness from your sins, that you are cleansed from sin, and then, after you ask The Lord Jesus Christ to forgive you of your sins, you ask The Lord Jesus Christ to come into your heart and life, and he does right then and there.

I believe in water baptism by complete immersion under water, and in "The Holy Bible", it says that John the Baptist baptized Jesus Christ.

I believe in the virgin birth of The Lord Jesus Christ, and that Jesus Christ was sinless, and that He lived a sinless life, while He was in the form of a man, and that He taught people about God the Father, Himself, and The Holy Spirit, and He performed many miracles, and gave up His life for our sins.

I believe that Jesus Christ arose from the dead, and after seeing, and talking with many witnesses; He ascended up to Heaven, and is seated at the right hand of God the Father.

I believe that Jesus Christ will personally return to the earth someday, as king and power and glory, and that Jesus Christ The King and Lord Savior will reign and rule for thousands of years.

I believe that at the time Jesus Christ comes in the clouds of Glory, to return to the earth to reign as King Jesus Christ and Lord, the rapture of the church will take place.

I believe that someday, both saved people, and lost people will be resurrected, and they will both give account for their lives before God, and the saved people will go to life with Christ Jesus Lord and Redeemer, but the lost people will go to Hell fire and brimstone, and I pray that nobody goes to Hell, however, many people will chose to go to Hell.

I believe in The Holy Spirit, and that the Holy Spirit is the third person in The One God, and that The One God has always existed in three persons, God the Father, God the Son, and God the Holy Spirit, and that it is through The Holy Spirit that men are drawn to The Lord Jesus Christ, and that it is through The Holy Spirit that dwells in the believer's life that enables them, to live a Holy life unto God.

I believe in the baptism of The Holy Spirit, and I do speak in tongues, when it is appropriate, and I want anything, God has to give me, and I am grateful for God's blessings.

I believe that part of The Lord Jesus Christ's work, was in healing people both of physical and mental sicknesses, because By His stripes we are healed, and I have been healed many times in my lifetime, and my children and family have been healed many times in their lifetime.

I believe that many times throughout my family and my own life, unintentionally, we have drank or eaten poison, because we do not know when there has been poison sprayed on food or surfaces, where food is prepared that we have eaten, and we do not know when we have eaten spoiled foods, or contaminated foods and drinks from insects, even so, God has protected us.

I do believe, and have experienced many miracles in my lifetime, and I expect many more miracles, but I believe that if you pick up a snake, it may bite you.

My little girl, Mary Rachelle, called me at work, one time, during the middle of the night, and in a hysterical voice she said that her sister's python snake was out of its cage, and it was lost in our house. Believe you, me, I was so agitated that my oldest daughter had a python or any other kind of snake in our home that I was willing to run to my baby daughter's aid. I would have picked up that python in a minute, knowing that God would take care of me to save my baby.

Instead of leaving work, to rescue my little eleven-year old daughter, Rachelle, from the python snake that was at least three feet long, *dumb me,* I calmly asked my little baby, if her sister or brother was at home with her. She told me that her sister was at work because she worked nights, and her brother was asleep, and he did not want to be disturbed.

"Honey, wake up your brother, and tell him the snake is out of its cage. If he doesn't get up right now, I want to talk to him." I told Rachelle, in a low voice, so I would not disturb anybody around me at work. But a co-worker, who was, also, a nurse on duty with me that night, over-heard the conversation that I was having with my little daughter.

My nineteen-year old daughter, Mary Michelle, worked two jobs, she worked at Sears and Roebuck, and she worked nights as a desk clerk for a motel, and both of the jobs were in Danville, where we lived. Also, Mary went to college fulltime, and she got the python snake from her dad for Christmas three years earlier. Because it meant so much to her, I hated to tell her to get rid of it, so she kept it in a cage in her bedroom. Her bedroom door was usually shut, and the snake never got out before, and I was too busy to worry about it, *dumb me.*

One of the nurses who was working with me that night, was listening to me talk on the phone to my daughter, Rachelle, as she was telling me about the python snake being out of its cage, and that it was lost in our home. So the nurse wanted me to tell her about the snake, but I motioned for the nurse to answer a call light, while I waited for my little, eleven-year old daughter to get back to me, and tell me if her brother got up from his sleep to help her.

That was fast, because I could hear my twenty-two-year old son, Mike, consoling his little sister, Mary Rachelle, so I went back to work taking care of critical patients, for the rest of the night.

After I got home the next morning, Mike had gotten Mary Rachelle off to school, and he was at work, and my oldest daughter, Mary, who owned the python snake, was at the junior college in town. I was exhausted, so I took my shower without thinking about the snake, *real dumb me.* Then after my shower, I walked barefoot around the house, as I was looking for the snake.

I spent hours looking in Mary Rachelle's bedroom, and in her closet, and I ran my hands around, and through most of her clothes and bedding. I looked through her toys and books, and I, even, put my face under her bed, and crawled under it to see if I could find the python snake, before it bit my little girl.

Then I looked under my bed, and I looked in my bed, because Mary Michelle's bedroom was right across the hall from my room, and it was right across the hall from her little sister's room. The cage that the python snake was always in, unless Mary Michelle was holding it, was empty and the cage door was open.

I knew that I needed to get some sleep, so I could study for school. I was so exhausted from working all night and then looking for the snake, so I knelt down in front of my living room sofa and prayed. I cried out to Jesus for a miracle that He would protect us from the snake, and I prayed with many tears that God would let the python snake be found, before I had to leave for work that night.

I never thought about the miracle that God had already been doing, like protecting my children from the snake, the entire time, it lived in our home.

I never thought about how God had been protecting me from the snake, when I was looking for it. I certainly did not know that God was doing a miracle, right then and there, and that God was protecting me from getting bitten by the snake that was right there next to my knees. While I was down on my knees in front of the sofa crying so hard, and praying to God for a miracle, I did not know God was doing a miracle, right at that time that I was crying out to Him in prayer.

I was so exhausted and weak that I let The Holy Spirit fill me with His tongue, and speaking in words known only to our Lord; I lie down on the carpet next to the sofa and fell asleep for a few minutes. Then when I sat up there was a cold, slimy lump against the back of my neck, but I was so tired that I paid no attention to it, so I went to my room. I certainly did not think about the python, as I fell across my bed, and went to Lully-land.

After a few minutes, I woke up with a start, because I remembered the snake. I still wanted a miracle, before my little girl, Rachelle, would get home from school, because I could not go to work, if the snake was still not found.

Well, I would just have to quit work, and I would even quit school, because I would not leave my little daughter, Rachelle, and my other children, Mike and Mary, alone in our home again with that snake, so I decided that I would call the police.

With that decision in mind, I once again, as usual, walked barefoot, and started to go into the living room, and suddenly, I saw the python snake laying in the same spot in front of the sofa, where I had been on my knees praying to God for a miracle. God had been protecting me from the snake, the entire time that I had been looking for it.

At the same time that I saw the snake, Mary Michelle came into the living room from the opposite end of the room from where I was. She had just come in from work, and she was exhausted, and she did not know that her snake had even gotten out of its cage.

She put her purse down on a chair, and hurried to her snake. I think she was the only person I ever saw pick up that snake, and I used to see her with that snake wrapped around her little body and neck. It always made me aggravated when I saw that snake, especially, when I would see her holding it. The first time I saw the snake it stuck its tongue out at me, and every time I ever looked at it after that, it would stick its tongue out at me, and I never, ever, ever liked it.

Well, I became the most unpopular, unlikable mom in the world to my daughter that night, because I made the decision that the snake had to leave our home right then and there. Mary could put it in the garage for one night, and then the snake had to be out of the garage and off our property by the next evening.

I told her, "Get that snake out of this house, Mary".

Mary angrily told me, "What, how can you say that! Dad got me this snake for Christmas one year, and I'm not getting rid of it! My poor snake is so hungry that it's not moving very much, and if I put it in the garage, even for one night, it will get too cold and die".

She had that python snake as a pet, and I did not think anybody in the family liked it, but her, and I always knew it was a dangerous pet to have. Although, I never went against her dad when he made a decision, because he used to be the boss, but now, I realized that I was the boss in this home, because he was no longer here, because he was in Heaven.

Mike came home from work, and he brought his little sister, Rachelle, home from school. I called a family meeting, and I announced that I was now the boss of our home, and I apologized to any of my children that might feel like, I needed to have realized that before then.

I said that I was going to set rules, and rule number one, was that no snakes would ever be allowed in our home again. The python was out, as of right then, but it could stay in its cage in the garage, for ample time to sell it, or give it away.

Mary Michelle said, "If my snake has to leave, then I'm going to leave."

I said, "Get packing then, because the snake is out of this house right now. Your little sister could have gotten bit last night, or Mike could have been bit, because that snake is dangerous, and I will not take a chance on it ever getting out of its cage in this house again. In fact, I do not like the idea of its being in the garage, or any place else on this property, because it could get out and hurt anybody, and it might even come back inside this house, and I have never approved of that snake, being anywhere around this house".

Mary took the cage with the snake, and all of its stuff out to the garage, and she said the snake would get cold in the garage, so she put a warm towel in the cage for it to be on. Then she put it on a shelf in the garage, and stayed with the snake and felt bad, until she had to go to work that night.

The snake died, and of course, Mary blamed it on me, but that was just one of those things that came with being a mom, and I could take the blame. At least Rachelle did not get bit, and nobody else got bit, and that was the most important thing to me. God only knows that, my decision to get rid of the snake, or at least to get the snake out of the house into the garage that was part of the house, could have kept Mary Michelle from getting bitten, or strangled by the python snake.

However, God did not let me be in control of His plans for our lives, and I should have been praying Psalms 119:35, in "The Holy Bible". "Direct me in the path of Your Ways, for there I find delight!

Make me walk in the path of Your Commandments, for I delight in it."

I had no idea that God would entrust to me, any other husband besides Michael, or, any other children. However, God has given me a heart and soul so full of love that I have loved my other children. God did not give me more than I could bear, because God knows just how much we can bear, and He never gives us more than that. God gave me a son, Grant Alden Reed, and then a daughter-in-law, Cindy Reed, and grandsons, Isaac Levi and Caleb Ethan Reed. I stand on the Promises of God my Savior and Lord Jesus Christ, and God, The Father and The Holy Spirit of God. (See pictures of Grant and family at the end of my book.)

In John 15:8 through 17 it says:
"By this My Father is glorified,
That you bear much fruit; so you will be my disciples.
As the Father loved Me, I also have loved you; abide in my love.
These things I have spoken to you, that my joy may remain in you,
And, that your joy may be full. This is my commandment,
That you love one another as I have loved you
Greater love has no one than this,
Than to lay down one's life for his friends
You are my friends if you do whatever I command you.
No longer do I call you servants,
For a servant does not know what his master is doing;
But I have called you friends,
For all things that I heard from My Father I have made known to you.
You did not choose me, but I chose you and appointed you
That you should go and bear fruit,
And that your fruit should remain,

That whatever you ask the Father in My name He may give you
These things I command you, that you love one another."

I stand on these promises from Jesus Christ my Lord and Savior. I give Him all the Glory and Praise and Thanks for all that He has given to me, and I am thanking Jesus Christ, The Son of God, my Lord, and Savior, for giving me the trust of being the mother to all these His Children right here and now.

Thank You, Lord Jesus, with all of my soul and heart, for trusting me with these your children. Lord God, above all else may You, Lord God, keep Your Holy Spirit upon me, as I do your will for my life, and keep myself as the Godly mother that You, Lord God, want me to be. For I know without a doubt, it is your will for my life to be in prayer for these, your children, and to love them with your love that Your Holy Spirit has put upon me, I thank You, Lord God, for these gifts of Love.

16—Too Young to Die

◇◇◇◇◇◇◇◇◇◇◇◇◇◇◇◇◇◇◇◇◇◇◇◇◇◇◇◇◇◇◇◇◇◇◇◇

My son, Mike, helped me with Michael when I needed to take him to the emergency room at the hospital that was only a couple of miles from our home, where doctors had to stop and restart my husband's heart, because it was so irregular that it was destroying itself. Then Michael was signed up with hospice at the first of the year, and our son needed to go out of town where he was trained for a job that he got with the state.

I was in my third year of college, and Mary Michelle was going to Danville Area Community College, and Rachelle was in the fifth grade. Michael was at home in the care of hospice nurses that came to our home on a daily routine, and somebody always needed to be in our home taking care of my husband, at all times, or he would have to be in a nursing home facility. He did not, ever, want to be in a nursing home, so we were able to keep him at home.

Often, his parents would come to our home and stay with him, while I was in college, and then different men from The Assembly of God Church would come and stay with Michael, while I was in college.

Michael would tell me that he was afraid to die because he was afraid that I would forget about him and the kids would forget all about him, and people would forget about him as though he never existed. But I would always assure my wonderful love, my husband, Mike, that I would never forget him and I could not live without him.

Michael would tell me that he just knew if he died, I would lose our house, and somebody would be mean to me and hurt me, because he knew me well enough to know that I would always let everybody hurt me, and I would never say anything.

Then on May 5, my husband, Michael, was taking his own shower, and he was so exhausted that he lay down on our bed to rest. And the hospice nurse, Ina, came and did a physical on him, as usual.

After Ina left, Michael was resting on our bed and he asked me play the piano and sing for him, because his head hurt, so badly, that he thought it would help him relax, so I played the piano and sang. Almost every time I sing, I cry because I sing to God, so I was crying and tears were falling onto the piano keys. So I stopped and blew my nose and wiped the tears off my face and off the piano keys, and my husband said he wanted me to keep on playing and singing, because that was helping his head feel better, so I kept on trying to.

However, I cried so much that I would need to stop and blow my nose and wipe the piano keys off, again and again, as I played the piano and sang and cried, I kept on praying singing prayers, that I do most of the time when I'm worshiping God. And I prayed to Jesus, as I sang and wept for my husband's healing.

And, I laid my head down on my piano and cried and cried, my heart was broken in a million pieces because I could not stand to have my husband sick. Throughout our marriage, I used to pray and pray for my husband to get well from that awful, melanoma cancer that he was battling. I hated it that my husband was sick, and he was the only lover I had ever had in my life.

Then I tried to encourage my husband to eat his favorite meal that I had prepared for him, as I fed it to him because he just laid on our bed, but he pushed the food away.

Michael said, "I can't eat anymore, because I have to play ball tonight. How do you expect me to eat very much, when I have a ball game in a little bit?"

With that statement, I knew that my husband was without a doubt getting sicker, because of course, he did not have a ball game, he was too sick to play ball. Although, Michael was still saying, "I have a ball game to go to, so I can't eat, anymore!"

So I set the food back on the tray that was still on the chair next to the bed where Michael was laying. I had been holding the plate of food on my lap, while I sat on the bed next to my husband when I was feeding him. He always liked my mashed potatoes and beef and noodles, so I was kind of surprised that he was not eating more of them.

Also, I was surprised that Michael was even lying down for so long, because this was not at all the way my husband was, to take a nap during the afternoon. Even though, Michael was in the care of hospice, I never gave him up to die.

Nobody actually thought that my husband was going to die for a real long time, because at six foot four inches tall, he still maintained his weight of 235 pounds. Although he may have lost some weight, because our youngest daughter, Rachelle, said she was sure he had lost a lot of weight. And for the most part, Michael did all of his own activities of daily living, and he certainly, fed himself every time he ate.

Before I took the tray of food into the bedroom, I had gone in there and told my husband that supper was ready. And it was about five o'clock in the evening, and that was the time we almost always ate supper, and our son, Mike, was away from home taking training for a job that he was getting with the state, so he was not at home.

Our two daughters, Mary Rachelle and Mary Michelle, were not at home at the time, because Mary Michelle was working at Sears and Roebuck, and Mary Rachelle was studying across the street at her friend, Megan's house. And my husband did not get up from the bed to come into the kitchen and eat. So I had gone over to the bed and looked at him, and I asked him if he wanted me to bring his supper in to him.

My husband had not said anything to me, and I knew he would not like it if his food got cold, so I fixed the tray of food and took it in to him. But he did not sit up to eat, and I had a hard time trying to put pillows under his head, so he could eat in bed. And although this was the first time he was going to eat in bed, he did not even try to help me lift his head to get it propped up on the pillows.

However, once I saw that his head was propped up enough that he could safely eat, I gave him a drink of tea. And he did not even try to hold his hand up to take the glass, so I held the glass up to his mouth for him to drink, and he did. And then he did not try to put his hand up to take a hold on the fork, so I fed him food with his fork, and my husband was not making any effort at all to feed himself.

I thought, "Okay, that's enough, we moved here to Danville to be close to family, and I am going to call Mike's parents and have them come over here and help me with my husband".

So, with that, I called his parents phone number, but nobody answered. And I realized it was already after seven o'clock by then, and of course, our youngest daughter, Rachelle, was home at five o'clock because she knew we ate then. And she looked for her daddy and me, because we were not in the kitchen, and when she saw me in the bedroom with her daddy, she had gone on ahead and fixed herself a plate of the food and eaten.

Since I realized all of our families on both Michael's side and mine were at church already, I called the church. I gave a message to the person in the church office that my husband was really sick, and I wanted his family to come and see him. I also told that the person on the phone that my husband was sicker than I had ever seen him, and I was going to call the hospice nurse, as soon as I got off the phone from them.

The hospice nurse that came right over was a young lady that had never taken care of my husband before that night. I told her that I wanted Ina, the registered nurse who always came to our home and took care of my husband, or I would be satisfied if Ina could not come for her to get Sally, another nurse who came on Ina's days off.

However, this young registered nurse let me know that neither Ina nor Sally could come to our home that night, because it was after eight o'clock in the evening before she came, and about the same time, Michael's parents came, and his sister, Jeanie, and her husband, Keith, and their children, Jennie, Raymond and Anthony, came. And Michael's brother, Tom, and his wife, Marilyn, came and Pastor Rogers of The Assembly of God Church where we were members came.

There were a lot of family in our home, and Mary Michelle and I had final exams that we needed to study for that we were going to have the next day. However, neither one of us could get any studying done because Michael was so sick that night. And the young hospice nurse kept assuring all of us that he was going to be all right.

Michael was my husband and I had never seen him that sick before, and I took his vital signs every fifteen minutes. His heart rate was so fast that I could not really count it, because its rhythm was irregular and it was over 100 beats per minute. Also, his blood pressure would be 160 over 110 and then it would drop down to 70 over 30, and then it would go back up to 180 over 140. And his blood pressure was that irregular, and his respirations were shallow and labored, to where, Michael's breathing sounded like a balloon that was ready to pop from too much air going into it.

We could hear a deep groan with every breath that he took, and he needed oxygen, but he was refusing treatment that night. And the young nurse insisted that she was in charge of him, and for me to let her do the hospice nursing job that she had a lot of experience doing. She did not think my husband needed oxygen, and she thought he needed to be left alone, so he could get some sleep, and she thought I was just being paranoid, because she did not think he was as bad off as I was insisting.

My husband said, "No, you leave me alone, I'm not going to the hospital, just leave me alone, I want Ina, Mary, if you don't call Ina for me, give me the phone and I'll call Ina".

I called the number that Ina had given me to call her anytime day or night. However, Ina was at a home where a man was dying, and she could not leave him. And Ina told me that she would come to our home the first thing in the morning, or even later that night, if that man was stable enough for her to leave him.

The young hospice nurse stayed until after midnight, and took vital signs every fifteen minutes. She would tell all of us that Michael's vital signs were normal. I would take them either before or after she took them, and they were not normal at all. So I would tell that hospice nurse what I heard, and she would tell me that I was just a student in college, and I was wrong and she was right.

She would tell us that she had experience with people like Michael, and she was a registered nurse, and what she heard was normal. She said for all of us to take her word that Michael was doing all right. And she would say that it did not matter what I said, when I told her that I knew what I was hearing when I took my husband's vital signs, and he needed a doctor.

This hospice nurse debated with me that, since Michael was in the care of hospice, a doctor was not needed. She was a hospice nurse could make the decisions about what the patient needed. And she said that my husband looked healthy because he was a big man, and he would be all right, and still be here in the morning.

Then, Ina, the hospice nurse who always came out to take care of Michael would be at our home, and she could take care of him. And she insisted that my husband was tired and needed a good night sleep, because it showed in the records, which she had on him from Ina, that Michael was only getting about two to four hours of sleep a night.

Then this young hospice nurse told everybody that it was getting real late because it was after midnight, and Michael would still be here in the morning. She made a cross symbol over her heart with her right hand, and said that Michael will still be here in the morning. He just needs a good night's sleep, because he didn't sleep very much at night, and that Michael was exhausted.

So she had given him a morphine table that would help him relax and sleep. She told everybody that she was going home, and Ina would be out the first thing in the morning. Then this young hospice nurse suggested to everybody that they all go home for the night.

Before everybody went home, I told them to each take a turn, and tell Michael whatever they wanted to, so he would know that they had all come to see him that night because he was so sick. They all did, and everybody took a turn, and went into our bedroom where Michael was laboring to breathe, while he was lying on our bed.

Jeanie and Keith, Anthony and Raymond, and Jennie, and Tom and Marilyn, and Reverend Rogers all went into our bedroom one or two at a time and told Michael that they were there, and they loved him, and they all told him that they would see him.

Michael's mom and dad went into our bedroom, and his dad laid his hands on Michael, and prayed real hard in his loud voice, out to God to heal his son. And Michael's dad, Eugene Proctor, told his son, my husband that he was healed, and he was crying and Michael's mom, Hazel Proctor, was crying like she always did when she was sad.

We were sad because Michael was so sick, and all of us were all very concerned and worried because my husband was laboring to breathe so much. However, this young hospice nurse said that he did not need oxygen because his breathing was not that labored.

The young hospice nurse insisted that Michael would be all right, and that everybody needed to go home and let him sleep. After a good night sleep, Michael would be better in the morning, because she insisted to Michael that he needed to take the morphine pill, that he was supposed to be taking all along, throughout his hospice care, which was going to take effect and make him sleep. Also, it was going to cause Michael not to be in pain, because the morphine pill was prescribed for pain.

The young hospice nurse said that Michael was breathing the way he was, because he was in pain. The morphine pill that she gave him was to take the pain away, and once the pain was gone, Michael would be able to sleep. However, I still insisted that my husband never looked so pale, and his skin was very slimy feeling, and his vitals were very irregular.

To me, my husband looked like he was having a heart attack, and I kept on telling this hospice nurse that. But she kept getting aggravated at me, and telling me to let her do the hospice job that she knew how to do. And she would tell me that I was not a nurse yet, because I was still a student in school, and I did not have any experience with patients like Michael. And I needed to stop telling her that I heard something different than she did. And I needed to stop taking my husband's vital signs, because she was taking them.

I still stayed right in the room with my husband, and I still took his vital signs. And I had my little daughter, Rachelle, sit at her daddy's head where his pillow was, and keep washing his forehead with a cool cloth. And she did that for the entire evening, until everybody went home.

Then I told Rachelle that she needed to be in bed, because it was after midnight. It was going to be very hard for her to get up in the morning for school. We always tried to make sure our children were in bed early on school nights, and I felt bad that our little girl was going to bed so late that night.

Mary Michelle had come home from work that night, and she had a research paper that needed to be done. So she kept trying to work on that, and a final exam that she was going to have. However, there were so many people at our home that she, just, had to give up, and there was no way she could study with all of the noise going on, even when she was in our finished basement.

There was so much stress in our home because Mary Michelle's daddy was so sick that she came into our bedroom to be of help. She also kissed her daddy and told him that she was sorry he was so sick, and she told her daddy that she loved him very much, and she cried because her daddy was sicker than she had ever seen him before.

Although, once before her dad was signed up with hospice, he was having chest pains, and he would not let me call the hospital, and take him to the emergency room. So, our son, Mike, helped me dress his dad and get him, against his protests into the car, to take him to the emergency room at the hospital. And that was where Michael was put into a cardiac area of the emergency room, and I waited at my husband's bedside.

At that time, I told my husband that I wanted him to live and stay with us, and he needed to stay alive and help me raise our children that needed both of us. Then I kissed my husband tenderly, before I was shooed out of the room, because a cardiac doctor was going to stop Mike's heart with electrode paddles that were designed to do the procedure. And then it would restart because his heart rhythm was irregular to the extent that the doctor said it was destroying my husband.

After the first procedure was over, this same cardiac doctor came out into the hall where I was standing with some of our children, and he told me that the shocks to my husband's heart did not help his heart start beating with the rhythm that he needed, in order to live very long. And that meant my husband was going to die, if he left him in the condition that his heart was in. Then the cardiac doctor let me go into the room to see my husband, before anybody else got to see him.

Michael was lying on the bed in the cardiac emergency room of the hospital, and his face was completely pale and slimy, and he was not moving, at all. And the cardiac doctor told me that the lines on the monitor next to the bed showed that Mike's heart was too irregular to keep him from dying in a few minutes. So I panicked and got as close as I could to my husband.

And, I yelled loudly into his ear. "Mike Proctor, you come back here, right now, because you are not going to die, and leave me alone to take care of our children, all by myself! Mike Proctor, I love you, and I cannot live without you! Mike, come back here! Oh, God, please, make my husband come back to me, because we need Mike! He is the father of our children, so Mike Proctor, come back to me, because I love you!"

Then, the cardiac doctor came back into the room where I was yelling into my husband's ear. For a nurse had told me to be quiet, and she tried to pull me away from my husband, but I did not listen to her, and I did not let her pull me away, because I held on to the rail of the bed that he was in. Then the cardiac doctor told me he could use the electrode paddles on my husband again, if I would sign a paper that gave him permission to do so.

Immediately, I signed the papers, and I was ushered out into the hallway, where I again waited with our son, Mike. This time the cardiac doctor did the electrodes at 100%, and Michael's heart stopped and restarted, and he lived. And I Praised God, because my husband was alive, and he came home to live with us, after a few days in the hospital.

I was told that there was extensive damage done to my husband's heart, when his heart had to be stopped and restarted two separate times. And Michael had damage to his brain, because of his heart stopping and being damaged, because no oxygen was going to his brain for a significant amount of time. And that caused my husband to be different, because he never recovered from the heart damage, and the brain damage that happened when his heart stopped. Also, after that his heart was always irregular, and his blood pressure was always, either too low or too high.

He was given medicine to try and help regulate his blood pressure, and medicine to try and regulate his heart rhythm. And my husband was also given morphine pills to try to control the pain that he complained about being extremely unbearable. And of course, Michael was given nitroglycerin pills to put under his tongue when he had chest pains, or any time he felt like his anxiety level was getting out of control, and causing him not to be able to breathe easily.

Then Michael was signed up with hospice care, and he got to be at home, and two registered nurses shared the responsibility of his care, and they were Ina and Sally. However, Ina was the nurse who was usually at our home giving Michael physicals and over-seeing his medications. Although, Michael was taking his own medicine after he came home from the hospital, because he would not let me be in charge of his medicine, or anything about his care.

He was very angry with me, because he told me that he heard everything that I was saying when he was in the cardiac emergency room at the hospital. He told me that he heard me telling him to get back here, and not to die and leave me alone, so I would have to raise our children without him. And he told me that he could hear me yelling, and it sounded like I was real far away in some distant land. And he heard me yelling that I love him, and I could not live without him. And he heard me begging God to make him come back to me, and help me take care of our children, because we could not live without him.

That caused my husband to be angry towards me, because he said he liked where he was going, and he did not have any pain at all, but now he had unbearable pain, all of the time, and he liked the cool freedom that he had when he was floating up on a cloud, where he could see bright lights far away from him.

He could feel himself floating up and up, and he wanted to be without pain, and my husband said that I was so selfish that I would not stop calling him, and he heard me pleading with God to make him come back, and here he was back with me, and he told me that because I was so selfish that I made him come back, because I loved him too much to be without him, he had to be here in agonizing pain, and I was truly so sorry that my husband, Michael, was in all of that pain, and I cried and cried, as I held my arms around him, and I was very glad that he let me hold him close to me, even though, he was in a lot of pain.

Michael had permanent damage done to his heart, however, if the cardiac doctor had not done the procedures that he did in the cardiac emergency room of the hospital, my husband would not have lived through the next few hours, and at that time, Mike's blood pressure was 60 over 10, and the doctor could not find a pulse, even with a stethoscope.

Well, shortly after the young hospice nurse told all of our family to go home, after midnight on May 6, 1993, my husband died!

Michael was only 44 years old, and he weighed 235 pounds, and he was born on May 22, 1948, to Hazel Eileen Hobbs Proctor and Eugene Emmett Proctor in Danville, Illinois, and he had a brother, Tom, and a sister, Jeanie. Michael died in our home at 1141 Lake Ridge Road, Danville, Illinois 61832, and Michael was married to me, Mary Jane Dill Proctor, his wife for 22 years and 10 months, and we had three children together, Michael Dean II, Mary Michelle, and Mary Rachelle. Michael Dean Proctor died on May 6, 1993, at approximately 12:50 A M, and my husband went to Heaven, right then and there!

My son stayed home from his training for the new state job that he was getting, and helped with all of the funeral arrangements. He found a nice cemetery, Johnson's Cemetery, where I could have a big, head stone placed on the grave, and I ended up purchasing twelve grave plots because I got very good deals on all of them.

The casket was nice, but Mike and his Grandpa Proctor wanted an even better one, so they each put in some extra money for one that they wanted for Michael to be laid in. I encouraged my children to put any little things into their daddy's casket with him that they wanted to. So Baby Rachelle put her favorite panda bear that was named Tommy, after her favorite uncle, Tom Proctor, in the casket.

The visitation went okay, however Mike's birthday was the same day, May 8, so when Marilyn asked me if there was anything Tom and she could do, I told her that it was my son's birthday. I wanted to have cake and a get together for Mike, because I did not want my son to feel like he was forgotten on his birthday. Even though, I knew my son would not have cared, but I cared very much, that it was his birthday that day, on the same day that he was being kind and thoughtful, to guests that came to see his daddy on this visitation day.

So, Marilyn and Tom had a nice, surprise party for Mike in their home after the visitation was over, and it was very, good to see Mike, try to relax on his birthday. I felt very sorry for him that his daddy was in a casket on that day for everybody to see.

Then the next day was the funeral, and since I had encouraged our children to put anything into the casket with their daddy, one of the men on the Assembly of God Church softball team that my husband played on, gave me a ball with all of the player's signatures written on it that we could put inside the casket, just before the service started.

Then when a friend of our family was singing during the service for my husband, I lost it, but I had been trying so hard to be strong for our children. However, a burst of sobs came out of me, all at once, because my children were crying, and I could not stop crying.

We all four sat there, Mike on one side of his baby sister, Rachelle, and Mary Michelle on the other side of me. And we cried so much that everybody in that church could hear us over the singing, as Bill's voice rang out "If you could see me, now, standing on streets of gold".

Well, when Pastor Rogers gave the message, and talked about what a wonderful person my husband was, I sobbed and sobbed. Both of my daughters on both sides of me sobbed, and sobbed, and my son cried. We could not stop crying, and we tried to, but we could not stop, because we sobbed more than ever, when we tried to stop crying.

All of my family dropped everything they were doing, and even though they could not afford the trip, they all came to the visitation and the funeral. My sister and her husband, Linda and Mike Joplin, and their family came and visited us in our home, and they were the first ones on my side of the family that came to visit us. Although, my mom had stayed for the rest of the night after Michael died.

Some of my friends listened to me, as I told them how I felt like I could still hear my husband in our home, and, sometimes, I thought that I would see him. And that caused some of my friends to be concerned about me, because they talked about that several years later. However, some people do not understand that it is part of the grieving process.

When people who lose somebody that is very close to them, and they want their loved one to be with them so badly, sometimes they think the loved one is still with them. And they may imagine that they can see the person, and hear the person for several weeks, or, even months, or years, after they have died.

I could never explain that part of my grieving process to some people because they did not understand. And they just must have thought that the devil or demons or both were in my home, when I said that I thought I saw my husband and heard him the day after he died. I wanted him to be alive, so badly, and I wanted him to be in our home where he belonged with me. Although, I never saw Michael again, and I never heard him again, after he died.

My sister, Linda, and her husband and children, Mike, Nik, and Sara, and maybe, Rob, came to Michael's funeral, also, my sister, Betty, and her husband and son, Shawn, came. And my sister, Miriam and her husband, Jack, and their children, Jack, Cindy, Diana, David, and Kyle came, and my sister, Judy, and her children, Julie, Laura, and Adam came. Also, my sister Debbie, and her children, Nicki and Ryan, and my sister, Joy, and son, Travis, and my brother, Jim, and his girlfriend,

Nicky, all came. And, of course, all of my husband's family came, and all of the people from church, and the schools and work places all came, and it was a very big visitation, and a lot of people were at Michael's funeral.

The funeral was on a Sunday afternoon, and the funeral home did not dig graves and bury people on Sundays, so the burial for Michael had to be the next morning. Then that night I had nightmares that my husband's body was not buried, instead, it was used in anatomy to teach students about the human body parts.

In my dream, I was looking at Michael in one of the containers that cadavers were in that were in my Anatomy Class, and Michael jumped out at me. He grabbed me and threw me and hurt me so badly that I could not move. He kept telling me in my dream, that if I told anybody or tried to get away from him, he would find me and hurt me even worse than I could ever imagine.

And that caused me so much stress that I called the funeral home where my husband's body was in the casket, because I wanted to be sure, I knew without a doubt, that my husband was in his casket when it was buried on Monday morning. I also wanted to see my husband one more time before he was buried, even with Michael's body in the casket, it was very hard, for me to think that he was really gone.

So, on Monday morning, there was a private showing for Michael, and we got to go where Michael was at the funeral home. And my little, Baby Rachelle was worried about Tommy Bear being afraid, because he would miss her, so before we left, she asked me if it would be all right for her to trade a different bear that she had, and get her Tommy panda bear back. And, of course, that was all right with me, because Baby Rachelle was, and always will be so very precious to me, after all, she is my little miracle baby.

Then Rachelle went with Mike in his car, and Mary Michelle left with me in my car, and we were going meet at the burial plot.

Mary Michelle had not eaten any breakfast, so we ate at Hardees, and then she started crying, and I was trying real hard not to cry, since I was driving.

So, guess what, yes, we got lost, and neither one of us had ever driven out to Johnson Cemetery where the burial was going to be. And I had only been out there once, and that was when Mike had driven me around to decide where we wanted Michael to be buried. And we could not even remember the name of that cemetery that Michael was going to be buried in, and we were so stressed out that both of our memories went blank.

At least, I was able to think for myself, enough, that I stopped at the first place I saw, which was a grocery store. I told Mary Michelle to wait in the car, while I went inside and called the funeral home, to ask where the cemetery was. And then I started crying when I tried to use the pay phone in the grocery store, but there was a policeman, or maybe a security officer, in that grocery store who asked me, if he could help me.

I cried, as I told the policeman, "My husband died, and he is going to be buried in ten minutes, and I cannot find the phone number of the funeral home that is taking my husband to the cemetery".

The policeman asked me, "What is the name of the funeral home, and can you tell me the name of your husband?"

By that time, I was crying harder, so I could verily talk, but I managed, to say, "My husband is Mike Proctor the second, and it is Barrick & Son Funeral Home".

The policeman called the funeral home for me, and then he asked, "How did you end up in this grocery store?", although, by then, I was sobbing, and I could not tell him.

Then the policeman said, "I'll stay with you, until, somebody from funeral home gets here, because I called them, and they are on their way here to escort you".

As I was wiping my eyes and face, I said, "My daughter is in our car, and I can drive".

The policeman walked with me to my car, and my daughter thought something was wrong when she saw a policeman with me. However, the escort car from the funeral home came and I followed it to Johnson Cemetery, and Mary Michelle and I quickly got out of our car because everybody was already there. And we sat in the two seats next to Mike that he had reserved for us, in the front row next to himself.

I quietly told my son, "We could not find the cemetery".

He whispered, "I knew something was wrong, when you didn't come sooner."

I ordered a headstone that was in the shape of two big hearts. And I stayed up, until, all hours of that night after my husband was buried, as I thought about exactly what I wanted to have written on those hearts. One heart was over the head of my husband's grave, and one heart was over the place where my body will be laid someday.

I prayed and cried a lot that night, as I thought about what I wanted to say on those two hearts. Then it came to me, exactly, what needed to be written, and I made it all up with God in complete charge of what I wrote.

"Death is the Gateway to Heaven, we all must pass through, I am not in this grave, I have a brand new heavenly body, that I got right after I died, I saw you cry when I died, and I wanted to reach out to you, and tell you, "Do not cry for me, for I have a brand new body and I, am with Jesus, and all of our love ones who have come to Heaven before me, be happy for me, I am in my mansion in Heaven, and I am without any pain, and sickness, I am so happy, with my brand new life here in Heaven, and someday soon all our family will meet for that reuniting in the wonderful new home God has prepared for us!"

17—College and Work

My husband and I paid tithes and gave offerings to churches, and people who were very much in need. We gave out of the blessings that God gave to us, and we gave our all when we told Jesus that we would go anywhere He wanted us to go. Then we were sent way out west in the farthest parts of Kansas where we had never been, and where only God knew us.

Then we lived through storms and hail the size of golf balls, and winds that blew my laundry off the clotheslines into the neighbor's yards and into the dirt in the alleys. A lot of times, we never had enough money to buy gas for our car, but God always provided for us.

We did not have the money, to buy baby formula and baby food, and vitamins for me when I was pregnant. However, our God is aware of everything that His children need, and He provided every need that we ever had.

Our God is bigger than all of the needs in the world, and He owns all of the cattle on a thousand hills, and our God supplies all of our needs. I have always given, and always will give all the glory and thanks to God for supplying all of our needs.

God gives us many blessings, and I give God the thanks that He is so mighty good. I thank You, Lord Jesus, for supplying all of our needs, and for all of the many blessings that You, Lord God, have blessed us with all my life through. For every breath that I take is a gift from You, Lord God. I am here because You, Lord God, made me and you want me here, and You, Lord God, are helping me, as I write my book, "Abused, Conquered, Alive".

We believe according to The New Testament in "The Holy Bible" in Hebrews 7:8,

> Here mortal men receive tithes,
> But there He receives them,
> Of whom it is witnessed that He lives.

In the last book of The Old Testament, in "The Holy Bible" in Malachi 3:8-12, God says,

> "Will a man rob God?
> Yet you have robbed me,
> But you say,
> In what way have we robbed you?
> In tithes and offerings
>
> You are cursed with a curse,
> For you have robbed me
> Even this whole nation
>
> Bring all the tithes into the storehouse,
> That there may be food in my house,
> And try me now in this,
> Says the Lord of hosts,
>
> If I will not open for you the windows of Heaven
> And pour out for you such blessing
> That there will not be room enough to receive it
>
> I will rebuke the devourer for your sakes,
> So that he will not destroy the fruit of your ground,
> Nor shall the vine fail to bear fruit for you in the field,
> The Lord of Hosts says".

A lady name Kathy held my hand for a few seconds, as she passed in front of my children and me, where we sat in the four seats in front of my husband's casket. Kathy put a $100.00 bill in my hand that was all folded up. Although, my hands were full of waded up wet tissues, I felt the folded up bill, as she pushed it into the palm of my hand, and I thank my Lord and Savior for Kathy and her precious family, every time I think about that.

Although, I thanked this precious child of God for her gift of $100.00, I shall never ever be able to thank her enough. At that time, when my husband died I did not think we had any insurance, and I knew that we did not have any money.

I thought that we would need to depend on my son, Mike, to take care of us for a while, and I had no idea how I was going to pay for my husband's funeral, *but, I knew that I knew,* who is in charge of my family, and I knew for certain whose child I am, and Praise God, I am a child of The King!

Rachelle and I went back home where we lived at 1141 Lake Ridge Road in Danville, and there was a pile of bills from doctors and the hospital that had letters with them, which let my husband and I know that they were going to turn them over to collection agencies. Also, there were a lot of other unpaid bills that had piled up, and right after the funeral service was over, I had been handed a bill from the funeral home that was over $6,000.00, and I was told they expected it to be paid in full within thirty days. And I stacked all of the bills together in one pile on the kitchen table, and I laid my hands on top of all those bills.

I prayed, "Lord God, You took my husband, Michael Proctor, from me, and I know my husband is in Heaven with You, and I cannot pay these bills. I give every one of these bills to You, Lord Jesus, to pay for me, please, because now, You, Lord God, are my husband, in Jesus Name, I pray and I thank You, Lord Jesus".

After I prayed, I sat down at the kitchen table where I had piled all of those bills, and I started making phone calls to each number that was on the bills. One by one, I called every one of them, except for the funeral home, and that bill I would pay in full the next day with all of the money from our church family, and from all of the money that was in the cards that my daughters were opening at the dining room table. Also, I would use any of the money that was needed to pay a lot of bills that accumulated from the check for over $11,000.00 that was life insurance on my husband.

Yes, I stayed on the telephone and I prayed in my thought life that is in my mind, the entire time that I waited for somebody to come back to the phone, and because I believe that God wants us to pray in our spirit when we talk to Him, according to God's Holy Word. And nobody knew that I was praying, not even my children, Mary Michelle and Baby Rachelle, who were going through all of the sympathy cards that wonderful people sent to us.

Sometimes, I got to pray for wisdom from my Lord Jesus Christ, for as long as thirty minutes, before somebody would come back to the telephone. I have always valued any time that I can get, as time that I get to pray in my spirit to my Lord Jesus.

Well, by the time somebody would answer the phone, I was holding my breath, because I knew these were very big bills that I would never be able to pay, because only my Lord Jesus could pay these kinds of bills for me, because nobody had money like that.

The person would say, "Mary Proctor, I'm sorry your husband died, and you have my sympathy, about the bill, we have taken it off our records, so you don't need to worry about paying it, anymore".

Very calmly, I would say, "Thank you very much, and I keep good records, so I would appreciate it if you will, please, send me a statement showing that the bill is taken off our account, and that we have a zero balance, please".

The person would say, "Yes, I can do that, and I will have my nurse send you a statement today, and it will show that you have a zero balance, Mary Proctor. You are going to make, quite, an efficient nurse, and I'm sure that I will work with you before long. Again, I want to give you my sympathy about your husband, but you will make it, and just, keep on going to Lakeview College of Nursing".

Then I would say, "Yes, I am going to keep on going to Lakeview College of Nursing, thank you, good-bye", and that person would say, very kindly, "Good-bye".

Yes, thank You, Lord Jesus, yes, yes, yes, glory, well, Glory to God, Hallelujah, Praise the Lord, thank You, Jesus, I give You, Lord God, all the Glory and Thanks that You, Lord God, deserve, because You, Lord Jesus, paid this bill for me, and I thank You, Jesus, Hallelujah!

I was so thankful that our Lord Jesus paid bill after bill for me the rest of that day. And there were so many unpaid bills from years gone back, that I had to get paid. In God's Holy Word it says that He will be the husband to the widow, and I took God at His Words, because God was now my husband. And I let God pay all of those bills that were way over-due, from doctors and hospitals from the cancer surgeries and appointments, and medicines and all the things that my husband had to have done to keep him alive, for the eleven years that he battled with melanoma cancer.

Well, God was making a life for us in advance, when we launched out in faith that God had our family move to Danville, Illinois. And God had my life planned out for me, when Lakeview College of Nursing re-opened the year before we moved to Danville. And God caused me not to be able to find work, so I would end up going to college and becoming the Dynamic Nurse that He was turning me into.

However, college was the hardest thing I, ever, did in my life! I studied all the time, literally burying myself in my books. I worked and studied so much that I felt guilty a lot of times, because I am ashamed of myself for not cooling it enough to spend more time with my little girl, Rachelle. I was also working as much as I could in the med-surge unit of a hospital while I was going to college, and I put all of my energies into college and working, so I did not spend enough time with my baby.

Although, Rachelle and I sat together in the kitchen, and studied the Missionettes book together, because she was in the girls club that I taught at Covington Assembly of God Church that is called Missionettes. This was quality time alone with Rachelle, helping her with the projects in the girls club.

Then after about a year or so, Rachelle and another young lady, Torri, worked and studied so much, that they completed all the steps and memory work in this girls club. So at the age of twelve, Rachelle and Torri both graduated and a banquet was held in their honor. Then they had the highest honors in the Missionettes girls club, so they got to be honored with all of the other girls who graduated that year at the Assemblies of God campgrounds. So my son, Mike, took Mary Michelle and me to that big honor, and then he took us all out to dinner on the way home.

Many times, I have apologized to my little Darling Rachelle, and she is so precious that she, always, insists that I spent plenty of time with her. However, I have made sure I make time for my little girl every opportunity there is, but I was going to college full time and working outside of our home in hospitals and doctors' offices.

Then graduation day arrived, yea, and the graduation was going to be on May 15, 1994, which would have been the following Sunday. However, another graduation was going to be held in that church on the same day that my class was going to graduate. The Dean of our college had already ordered the certificates that said the graduation was going to take place on May 15, 1994, but the day needed to be changed, so we would graduate earlier.

So I was graduating from Lakeview College of Nursing on May 6, 1994, on a Sunday afternoon, exactly, one year after my husband died. And my husband's funeral was also on a Sunday afternoon, so that day was very sad for me. And I did not even want to attend my graduation because I wanted to stay in bed, and cry that day. But I got up and prepared to attend this graduation, because my children were excited that my big day had finally come. They knew I was sad, because we all felt lonely for their daddy, every time, any occasions came that he needed to be with us to help us celebrate something, too.

Then when it was my turn to go in front and get my diploma, my daughters yelled and hollered, saying they were so proud of their mommy. And I had no idea everybody that I had sent invitations to was at my graduation, except, for my husband's parents and sister who was sick. And the church was not big enough to have everybody's family and friends there, but my family and friends all were early and got seats.

The Dean of the Lakeview College of Nursing said, upon recommendation of the faculty of the college and the Board of Directors by virtue of the authority vested in it, hereby confers on Mary Proctor, the Degree of Bachelor of Science in Nursing Major in Nursing Practice, in recognition of the completion of the program of study prescribed for this degree, given at Danville, Illinois on Sunday, May 15, 1994. Then, Dean of the Lakeview College of Nursing said, Mary Proctor graduating Suma Cum Laude! And, she handed me a red rose.

Mary Michelle took pictures, and my daughters had a surprise party in my honor at our home. Then she invited all of our guests that came to my college graduation to come, too, and that was the most, precious, thing that any daughters could, ever, have done for their mommy in the whole, wide world. Of course, my son, Mike, was at my graduation, and he stayed for the party, and he was also very proud of his mommy.

I worked harder than I ever worked, or will ever work in my life, for my Bachelor of Science Degree. And I was so happy to see my children having a good time laughing and talking that day, when I graduated, and they had their surprise party in honor of me.

I was truly glad that I went to my graduation, because I would have ruined the day for them. And I would have ruined the day for all of the guests that came to honor me. And I thank God for helping me to have the strength, to get up out of bed that morning, and get a move on.

Although, I graduated from nursing school, I still had to pass state boards. People in my classes and friends in the community had been telling me to stop studying for boards, during the past six months before I graduated. However, if I did not pass the state boards in nursing, I would not be able to work as a registered nurse. So I kept right on studying, day and night, and the state boards test was on computers for the first time that anybody knew of. Before that year, the state board's tests were always on paper, and about six weeks after I had graduated, one of my good friends, Debbie called me, and invited me to go with her to take the state boards.

It was great, because God used Debbie and her wonderful husband to provide a ride for me. And God also helped me pass state boards the first time I took them. And I was afraid that something had gone wrong with the computer I was taking the boards on, because it shut off after about forty-five minutes. Then I patiently waited in a sitting room for the next two hours for my friend to finish taking the test, because we got two and a half hours to take it.

Words had come up on the computer after only forty-five minutes that said, "You have finished State Boards!"

Then I had to wait and see if I passed state boards, and that was very stressful. Then one day, I got an envelope in the mail from State Boards, and it was very stressful to even open it, because I was still studying to re-take the test. I did not have the confidence in myself that I might have passed them, so I prayed before I opened the envelope, just as I had prayed before I took the State Boards.

The paper inside the envelope said, "Congratulations, you have passed State Boards", wow, that made me very happy! Then I got my Illinois

State License to practice nursing as a registered nurse, which says, "State of Illinois Jim Edgar Governor Department of Professional Regulation This is to certify that Mary Proctor Has met all the requirements of the laws of the State of Illinois, and is hereby recognized by the Department to practice as a Registered Professional Nurse".

I worked for a Christian Nursing Agency, and I worked in a hospital, and I wanted to be a nurse practitioner in Gerontology. So I studied day and night to pass GRE, Graduate Record Exam, entrance exams in order to continue going to college, and I had gotten a scholarship to go to the University of Illinois, in Champaign, Illinois.

A couple of weeks, after I graduated from Lakeview College of Nursing, my daughter, Mary Michelle, graduated with an Associate's Degree in Business from Danville Area Community College. Then she moved to Terre Haute, Indiana, and attended Indiana State University for several months, and she was working on her Bachelor's Degree in Business.

However, both Mary Michelle and I were taking on too much in that we were both going to college and working so many hours at jobs. We needed to take time to grieve from Michael dying. So after a few months, we both quit going to college, and all three of my children and I lived together in our home that God paid for during the next few months.

Although, I worked more than ever at health care services that called me up, for emergency facilities that were in need of a registered nurse right then. And I was burning out because I was working almost all the time, and I was exhausted because I was not getting very much sleep. So, to keep from falling asleep, while I drove to and from work, I prayed a lot.

I had my nursing licenses for both Illinois and Indiana, because I worked in both states. I drove over 35 miles one way, to work at a hospital in Crawfordsville, Indiana, because that was my favorite place to work, at that time in my life. And since I had been working so much, I had a good savings account.

My home in Danville, Illinois, was paid for, and on my days off, my daughter, Rachelle, and I started looking at different homes that we thought might be something we would want to live in. And we were, actually, doing that because it gave us something to do that did not cost anything, and we were having fun together.

I was totally open to whatever God had for my children and me. And it turned out to be a funny thing, because Rachelle and I liked a house in Crawfordsville where I worked, so I made a bid on it. And this house had been on the market for months and months. Then the real estate lady came to the area where I worked in the hospital, and told me that another person placed a higher bid than I did and bought that house.

Well, Rachelle and I saw another house that we thought we might like to live in. And I bid whatever was being asked for the house. Then the real estate lady came to the hospital, and told me somebody bid over the asking price for that house. That house had, also, been on the market for months and months. And that happened the third time, after Rachelle and I found another house that we liked. And then this real estate lady that was working with me in Crawfordsville, Indiana, came to the hospital where I worked, and told me that she was *afraid!*

The real estate lady told me that she was a Christian, and she always asked God to be in control of her life and job. In as much as, she knew God was telling her and me something.

After three houses that had been on the market for so long, that I placed bids on in Crawfordsville, were all suddenly bought the day after I placed my bids, my real estate lady was *afraid* to work with me any longer. *The real estate lady told me that she knew, that she knew, that God was telling me something!* Furthermore, I needed to find out from God, if He wanted me to move to Crawfordsville.

I do not think that my son, Mike, realized that Rachelle and I had been looking at different houses, but Mary Michelle knew it, and sometimes, she would go with us for the fun of it. Actually, I had no real intensions of ever moving from my home that was all paid for on Lake Ridge Road in Danville, because it was very nice.

I was just spending time with my daughters, especially, with Rachelle, and she liked to look at different houses. And we always ate out together, and laughed about the houses that we saw. However, God was moving in my life, and I did not know that God was preparing me to like any other house, than the one He had paid for that we lived in when my husband was alive.

18—Home

I had my nurse uniform on, and I needed to leave for work, when my daughters, Mary Michelle and Rachelle, insisted that I go with them and look at two new houses on Winter Avenue in Danville. They knew I did not need to leave for Crawfordsville, where I worked in the hospital for at least thirty minutes, and my precious, little, daughters, Mary Michelle and Rachelle knew how to work their mommy.

They both came into our kitchen on Lake Ridge Road, and gave me their innocent looks, and they both said, "Mommy, can you, please, spend some time with us before you go to work, please, please?"

I could tell by looking at them that they had practiced this little thing of theirs, so I answered my daughters, and I said, "I have thirty minutes, so what do you have in mind?"

My youngest daughter, Rachelle said, "Mommy, there is a house on Winter Avenue that is for sale, and I can call the number that is on the sale sign, and maybe we can go and look at it".

As I looked into my little girl's pleading, big, blue eyes, I could see that she needed some of her mommy's tenderly, loving attention, so I smiled at her and replied, "Honey, there isn't time to look at a house, because I have to leave for work in thirty minutes, and besides that, I'm real tired".

I could hear my daughters talking about which one of them could get me to give in to them. Mary Michelle was telling Rachelle that she was my baby, and I would do anything that she wanted me to do, also, I had been spending a lot of time with her. Rachelle and I had been looking at a lot of houses together, and having fun together, so Mary

Michelle elected Rachelle to try to persuade me to look at those two houses with them.

Then Rachelle came up to me and smiled in her cute, little, innocent way, and pleaded, "Mom, can we at least call the number on the real estate sign, and set up an appointment to look at the house, because I have the number written down on a piece of paper".

With that my sweet, little daughter showed me a piece of paper they had written the phone number of the real estate lady on. Then Rachelle told me, if I did not like that house, there was a house a little closer to town that was on the same road that was, also, for sale.

I realized by then that I may as well give in to my daughters, because they already had their hearts set on looking at a house, so I answered, "Okay, but I need to leave for work in twenty-five minutes, now, Mary, you need to call and set up an appointment to see one or both of those houses, and just tell whatever real estate lady that you talk to, that your mom is too busy to talk right now, because I am getting ready to leave for work".

Then both of my daughters were screaming in delight, and they were really happy that I had given in to them, and then they came back to me, and Rachelle announced, "Mommy, the real estate lady is on the phone, and she said that she can meet us over at the first house that we want to see, right now, and then if you don't like that house, she can show us the other house right after the first one".

I was surprised by my daughter's enthusiasm, so I laughed and replied, "Okay, but tell her I have to leave for work in twenty minutes, actually, I don't have to leave that early, but I always like to leave for work a half hour early, in case something holds me up on the way there".

Rachelle and Mary Michelle were screaming with delight, because my two daughters were getting to do something that was fun with their mommy. I did not know God was using my two daughters, to put me in the center of His Will for my life again.

I drove my car, and Mary Michelle drove her car, so she could take Rachelle back home with her, because I would have to leave for Crawfordsville, Indiana, where I worked in the hospital, right after we looked at the houses, and that was if we had time to look at both of the houses.

Well, we pulled up at the first house, and the real estate lady was waiting for us, but I was very tired, and I did not like the first house at all, because it had all black appliances, and it was not big enough for our family. I wanted to leave for work, but my daughters asked me to, please, go and see the other house, because it was closer to town, but it was on the same road, as the one we had just looked at, and they wanted to see that house, and of course, they could not see it, unless I was with them, so I agreed, "Okay, but I will leave for work in ten minutes".

Mary Michelle followed the real estate lady in her car, and I followed the real estate lady in my car, so I could leave for work, and then as I was pulling up onto the lane of this second house that my daughters wanted to see, a strange thing happened to me.

A feeling came over me like I was in a trance, and I knew, that I knew, that this feeling was the Holy Spirit of God that was coming all over my body, because I had been praying to Jesus Christ for His leading. And I was so prayed up and over-flowing, with having been praying out loud to God, when I was driving to and from work, to all of those places that I was working. Then I was not getting very much sleep, with all of the hours that I was working and driving, and a lot of times I was having a hard time staying awake, *and, I knew, that I knew, that God's Holy Spirit was all over me!*

In as much as, I did not feel my feet touch the ground, as I opened the car door and got out. Praise God, I could feel God all over me, and it was a presence that I have felt many times in my life. And I could hardly breathe, because I felt like this was Holy ground that this house was setting on!

The real estate lady opened the front door of the second house that, I now felt like was setting on Holy ground, and I did not say a word. My two daughters went in before me, and they ran around inside this house, and then I felt my feet standing on the floor, and I knew that this was a Holy floor! And, I walked straight across the room and into the kitchen, and I stood at that kitchen sink, and then I looked across the room, and I saw a vision!

There was a table with chairs around it, and there was a wheel chair at one end of that table, and there were very, old women sitting in each chair, and an even older lady was sitting in that wheel chair. And I saw my two daughters, just as they looked that day, and I standing around this table helping those old women eat a dinner that was prepared on each one of their plates.

And without thinking, and without hesitation, this just came out of my mouth, as I looked at the real estate lady, and I said, "I will take this house for whatever the asking price is, because God will pay for this house within five years. God will pay me for taking care of, whatever he wants me to take care of, and I will become a millionaire within five years, because God has a work for me to do in this house, because this is God's house. And God will bless me, and my daughters in this house, so give me the form that needs to be signed, that I am buying this house."

That real estate lady just stood there in front of me and stared at me in amazement and my daughters had both come close enough to that kitchen to hear everything that I had said to that real estate lady. I believe, and I will always believe, that it was The Holy Spirit speaking through me, that said all of that to this real estate lady.

Mary Michelle and Rachelle were both screaming, and laughing at the top of their lungs by that time. And to the best of my recollection, this is what the real estate lady, may have, said something like this, to me, You can't do that, because you don't, even, know how much this house costs, and this house is a very, expensive house.

"Furthermore, I should not have, even, shown it to you, because for one thing, you haven't even seen the rest of this house, because you've only been in this kitchen, and you haven't even seen the rest of this kitchen, because there is a lot to this kitchen!"

"At least, let me show you the rest of this kitchen and the house, and then you have to be qualified for a loan. And you never give the asking price for a house, because you make a lower offer than the asking price, and go from there. And you cannot sign this form, because you cannot give these people their asking price for this house!"

Without hesitation, I replied, "I need to go to work, so give me the form, and I will sign it, and I will pay whatever the people want for this house."

Mary Michelle announced loudly, "You don't know my mom, because she prays to God all of the time. And my mom said that she will take this house, and God will pay for this house, and God will bless my mom, because God has always blessed my mom, so let my mom sign the paper. But Mom, don't you at least want to see the upstairs before you go to work?"

To the best of my recollection, the real estate lady may have been saying to me, Okay, you can sign the form, but this is not the way it's done, and you'll never get the loan for this house. The people that had this house built for them lost it to the bank, because this house is too, expensive.

"And, here you are, thinking that you can pay for this house, and you are a single widow woman. And oh, I just don't like it, but I will turn the form in that you signed, because by law, I have to give the sellers any offers that are made on the house."

"Don't you, at least, want to see the house before you sign your name for it, and let me write down an offer for you, because you can't just write that you will give them what they want, so I'll make it one that is realistic, so it doesn't look like you're, just, giving the sellers whatever they want, and oh, I don't like this, because business is not done like this!"

I continued to stand firm on what The Holy Spirit was using me to say, "God will pay for this house, and God will give them whatever it says on that form that the sellers need, because this is a Holy House, and this is God's House."

"This house has been prayed over many times, and this house has had tears unto the Lord Jesus, shed upon this land. And this house belongs to God, because the people who built this house gave it to the Lord Jesus, for His work before the foundations were ever laid."

I said all of this without, ever, knowing anything before that time, about this house that was truly the Lord's house. I was just letting The Holy Spirit speak through me, and I felt the presence of The Holy Spirit, so strongly, while I stood there in that kitchen talking to that real estate lady.

Then Mary Michelle and Rachelle persuaded me to run upstairs real, quick with them, to see that they both had already chosen their own bedrooms.

Then I told the real estate lady, that I would stop by her office first thing in the morning, at the address that was on a copy of the form that I had signed. And I left to go to Crawfordsville, Indiana, for work, and Mary Michelle drove her car with Rachelle in it back home.

Well, I prayed out loud to keep from falling asleep, and I thanked Jesus over and over, and I sang praises to His name, because that was what I always did when I went to work, and on my way back home from work every day and night.

I put the whole incidence behind me, as I worked hard all that night, and I did not tell anybody about it, because I never talked very much about my personal life, to my close friends that I worked with. And I considered it very important to always listen to their needs and desires, because they were my friends.

Then I got a surprising phone call at 8:20, the morning after I signed those papers, for those papers showed that I would take the house, on Winter Avenue that my daughters and I looked at, the afternoon before. And the call was from my bank, and the man asked me, if I wanted the house at 1017 East Winter Avenue, that I had signed my signature for, and I told him, "Yes", so the man at my bank said, "You've got it, but they have to get the asking price".

I politely answered, "Thank you, Sir, because God will help me, and the house will be paid for within five years for their asking price, because it will be my Lord Jesus Christ Who will pay for that house. And now, I need to get back to work, and I will stop by the real estate office that I signed the form for, after I get off work this morning, so thank you for calling, good-bye".

The man at the bank where I did all of my business, asked, "Can you stop by our bank, after you do your business at the real estate office?", and I answered, "Yes, good-bye".

Wow, and God had always been in control of my life, and God will always be in control of my life, and thank You, Lord Jesus, and, oh, how I thank You, Lord Jesus, because I am a child of The King!

My son, Mike, was on a vacation in Eudora, Kansas, at the time that I did the transaction to buy this house at 1017 East Winter Avenue in Danville, Illinois, and by the time he came home I already had made up my mind to sell our home on Lake Ridge Road. However, Mike was not a happy son when he met me at the door after I came home from work, because right after he got back from his vacation, my two daughters announced to him that we were moving to a new home.

I had, just, paid for the home that we were living in on Lake Ridge Road, and I had sold both of our family cars, and bought a red convertible and a brand new Oldsmobile family car, and now, I was in debt for a very, expensive house. Mike wanted to know how I planned to, ever, pay for that very, big new house, so I simply told my son that I knew it was God's will for me to have that house and the cars, and God would pay for everything, and I never doubted God, when I knew it was definitely my Lord Jesus that was directing me to do anything.

Since, God had helped me sell our home in Eudora, Kansas, I was sure that God would help me sell our home on Lake Ridge Road.

Our home on Lake Ridge Road was not selling, and all of my children and me, and my friend were taking care of the yard and home to keep it very nice. Then our family doctor suggested to me that it would be better for me to rent the home for the winter, rather than leave it vacant.

There was a new family that was moving to town that was going to come to the church that I was attending, when I was not working, and the family needed a home to rent. So it turned out that I rented my home on Lake Ridge Road to that family. Then, eventually, within a few months, I sold my home to that family.

God helped me with everything that I did, so my cars and house were all paid for. And I had all of the money from the sale of my home on Lake Ridge Road put on the new home that I was buying on East Winter Avenue.

By the time my home on Lake Ridge Road was sold, I was working taking care of women in my home on East Winter Avenue. Then, by the time that home had sold, I had been making enough money that I put more money with the sale of that home, to almost pay off my new home that my children and I were living in. Then within a few weeks, I was able to completely pay off the rest of the home at 1017 East Winter Avenue in Danville, Illinois, and I already had the big yard completely, professionally landscaped, and bought whatever my daughter wanted to help make it easier to take care of the yard.

The money came from the fact that I got paid for all of the work that I did. And I managed the money, very well, and all of these blessings were from my Lord Jesus, because I will never take the credit that is so very much due to God. I truly thank God for giving me the ability, and the wisdom to have the faith of a little child, and launch out into His blessings for my children and me, and God blessed us, although, we worked very hard, as God gave us the strength to do His Will for our lives.

By getting to stay at home and take care of women that could not take care of themselves, that gave me the golden opportunity to be at home all of the time for my children. This life was also especially good for Rachelle, because she got to have her mommy at home with her all the time. Although, Mary worked long hours at Sears and Roebuck in the mall, she always took care of the yard and helped me with the women that lived with us, and Rachelle, also, helped me every day when she was not in school.

The vision I had seen on the day the real estate lady showed Mary Michelle, Rachelle and I this house on East Winter Avenue that I bought, was a familiar scene in our home every day, because my two daughters and I worked real hard taking care of the very, old women that lived with us. One of the elderly women was in a wheel chair, and the others were able to walk with help to the kitchen table, and I always prepared their food on plates, that my daughters and I helped these very, elderly women eat. They were my family, and many of them accepted the Lord Jesus Christ into their hearts and lives, while they were right here in this kitchen.

It was a lot of work to take care of the elderly women who lived with my children and I, and complete strangers would beg me to let their parents and grandparents live with us, in order to get them out of nursing homes. All of these elderly women had needs, such as, one lady who was left at my home, by her daughter long enough for me to see, if I thought it would work out for her to live with me.

I was preparing dinner, and I had a big butcher knife on my sink where I was cutting up a large rump roast, and there was a pair of heavy, razor, edged, sewing scissors in a drawer of a white desk that matched all of the white cabinets in my immaculate kitchen. The visiting elderly lady who was sitting at my kitchen table must have gotten up and opened the desk drawer, and taken the scissors out without me seeing her. Then when I walked away from the rump roast with the butcher knife next to it, so I could wash my hands for just a minute, the elderly lady came over next to me.

Even though I was right beside the big butcher knife, the visiting lady grabbed it before I could reach for it, and, although, I asked her to, please, let me have the knife, she did not let go of it. Furthermore, she screamed at me and hit me with her arm, as she took a firm hold onto the knife. She was twice as heavy as me, and she was probably six inches taller than me; I only weighed 106 pounds, and I was only five foot three and a-half inches tall.

To keep from falling when this lady shoved me, I stepped back away from her, and then she stepped toward me, and I stepped back away from her again. Then I had to turn around and run because she held the big butcher knife in one hand and the large, razor, edged, sewing scissors in her other hand, as she chased me through one door after another in my home.

She was screaming at me, and I thought she was going to kill me, and, of course, I was telling her to stop, but she just kept right on chasing me, and I was afraid she was going to throw the knife and scissors at me. Then as I ran around the corner of my kitchen where the phone was on top of the desk, I grabbed the phone and kept right on running. I called for help, and I calmly talked to the lady to help her try to relax and stand still, although, she would not put the knife and scissors down, but at least she lowered them closer to the floor, and nobody else was in my home, at that time, so nobody got hurt.

The police came, and my brother and one of his big, strong friends came over to my home, and, at first, they could not get inside of my home because the doors were locked, but then as I was still running from this elderly lady who had the knife and scissors in her hands, I quickly turned the lock on the front door, so they could get inside.

Well, the lady was taken to a hospital, and, of course, I got over the whole ordeal, but I learned my lesson. I did not leave scissors or knives of any kind around where somebody might get hurt with them, anymore. The other thing I did was to make sure nobody left anybody in my home that did not, already, have their medication controlled.

I was happy that God helped me pay off this home at 1017 East Winter Avenue, in Danville, Illinois, and, of course, I wanted my daughters to have blessings, too, so in my mind I had been praying that God would use me to be a blessing to my daughters. Many of the blessings that God had been giving to me were the goodness and the joy that Mary Michelle and Rachelle gave to me every day. During their lives, I often prayed that God would use me to bless them every opportunity I had, and good things came into my mind when I prayed and asked Jesus to, please, use me to be a blessing to others.

One of my daughters had bills, from when she was in college that I asked her to give to me, so I could help her with them. And our bank was glad to loan me some money, and give me a lean on our home, which paid the bills. In turn, my daughter gave me a certain amount of money every month to put on the loan, which encouraged her, because I was able to put more with it, although, she had been paying me money every month to help with expenses. Now, it was my turn, to be used of God to bless my daughter, and my plan was to get all of my daughter's bills paid off, as soon as we could.

About the same time that I took a lean out on my home, which was already paid for, a good friend of mine called me that I knew from a hospital where I had worked in Champaign, Illinois, when I was working for an agency that sent nurses to places in need of a nurse for a few days.

My friend was desperate to have a place saved for her mother to go, because her mother was been diagnosed with Alzheimer's. So it was no surprise to me that she wanted me to let her mother live with me in my home, because she always called me "The Dynamic Nurse", because that was how much faith my friend had in me.

I guess, she thought that I could do almost anything that I set my mind to, or, at least, she said that almost every time she talked to me, and, of course, I would tell her it was all from God. I only did what I knew God wanted me to do, and it was God that gave me the wisdom to know how to do anything, and the strength to do what needed to be done.

Well, my friend worked out a deal with me, and she was going to pay me triple what everyone else was already paying. And she tried to give me gifts to reserve a room in my home for her mother, when the time would come that she had to be taken care of. With a great deal like that, and other deals that were being made with me to take care of loved ones, I was well on my way to becoming a millionaire. However, God was and always has been, in complete control of my life, and God had something else for me.

My life is in my Lord Jesus Christ, and I had taken Jesus Christ as my husband, after God took my husband to Heaven. And it was less than four years, since my husband, Michael, had died, and left all three of my children, Mike, Mary, and Rachelle, and me alone, crying.

Now, my life was completely different from when I used to worry about being homeless, and I was in the center of God's Will for my life. I did not need to worry about anything, at all, and I knew this new home belonged to God, so, I worked in it for God.

My twenty-six year old son, Mike, had moved into a place of his own because I needed his bedroom for the women that needed my nursing care, and needed a place to live. I let them come into our home on 1017 East Winter Avenue, so it was always full of family, and, of course, this included the family of elderly ladies, that I took care of with God in control, and the help of Mary and Rachelle, that I could not have done without.

More opportunities arose for my ministry, in opening my door to our new big home, as, unto the Lord Jesus Christ, and like Jesus says in "The Holy Bible" in Matthew 25:35 through 40,

> For I was hungry and you gave Me Food;
> I was thirsty and you gave Me Drink;
> I was a stranger and you took Me In;
>
> I was naked and you clothed me.
> I was sick and you visited me;
> I was in prison and you came to me.
>
> Then the righteous will answer Him, Saying,
> Lord, when did we see You Hungry and feed you,
> Or thirsty and give You Drink?
>
> When did we see You a Stranger and take You In,
> Or naked and clothe you,
>
> Or when did we see You Sick,
> Or in prison, and come to you,
>
> And the King will answer and say to them,
> Assuredly, I say to you,

Inasmuch as you did it to one of the least of My Brethren,
You did it to me.

Peace and joy were in my soul, as, I looked forward to The Lord Jesus working through me, to accomplish whatever He had for me to do for Him and His glory. I had faith in God, and I was open to anything that He let happen, so I was not surprised, by other phone calls that more, elderly ladies needed to be in my nursing care that would need to live with me.

I am a registered nurse with my bachelor of science experience that I used, as I worked with people who had Alzheimer's and dementia, and people who did not have knees and legs and feet, and who were crippled with diseases and could not walk, so they needed total nursing care. These were all of the needs of the elderly ladies that came to my door, and they lived in our new home. As I opened my doors to complete strangers who needed my nursing expertise, and all of the tender loving care that Mary, and Rachelle, and I gave to everybody that needed us.

Seeing the fruits of the Spirit of God in my children and me, drew many of them that had never repented of their sins, and asked Jesus to come into their hearts and lives to God. Then changes that came over these ladies became so dramatic, that their immediate families and friends that visited wanted to know what had happened, because some of the elderly ladies went from being, almost continually bitter and angry, to sweet and loving. Which was not the nature of some of the ladies, so that drew several other people who came to our home, to ask Jesus to take their sins away, and come into their hearts and lives as well.

For some reason or other, I just could not keep from talking about Jesus to people that came to my home, because they were on my territory that God was blessing me with. And some people in and around town were talking that nobody knew for sure who owned that home, because ladies who came to my home and wanted to live with me got to call me their nurse, if they wanted to.

My love and prayers for them and with them, and reading "The Holy Bible", and having Trinity Broadcasting Network on television for us to watch most of the time, got hold of them. And, believe you me, I love to talk about Jesus and all the wonders in "The Holy Bible", and all of the miracles that Jesus does daily, Praise The Lord, Hallelujah, thank You, Jesus, and I love You, Jesus, because God is so Good, and I thank You, Lord Jesus!

What an awesome ministry, and, oh, thank You, Lord Jesus, because how You, Lord God, expanded my territory, as, You, Lord God, did when Jabez said this prayer in first Chronicles 4:10, and Jabez called on the God of Israel saying, "Oh, that You would bless me indeed, and enlarge my territory, that Your hand would be with me, and that You would keep me from evil, that I may not cause pain!", so God granted him what he requested, and back in verse 9, it tells that Jabez's was more honorable than his brothers, and his mother called his name Jabez, saying, "Because I bore him in pain".

God's hand was truly with me in every job that I ever had, and, no way, could I have ever made it through my life, or anything at all, without God being with me, because I had been taught to be submissive by my parents and my husband and his parents. Instead of becoming angry and bitter, I let God use it in me to grow, and grow, and grow in the Fruits of The Holy Spirit of God, and they are found in Galatians 5:22-23. I have listed them for you: But the fruit of the Spirit is love, Joy, peace, longsuffering, kindness, Goodness, faithfulness, Gentleness, and self-control.

Circumstances that were out of an elderly lady's control, had caused her immediate family to sell the home and distribute her possessions. She had dementia and needed more help than I could give her, and she needed to go into the hospital, so I was seeking God for help, in regards, to letting her place in my home go to another lady.

Browsing through a newspaper, I saw an ad that said a man wanted a lady to take care of his wife that was presently in a nursing care facility. Although, the ad stated that he wanted a lady to take care of his wife in their home, I thought, maybe, he would like to consider my home for her, so I called the phone number that was part of the man's ad in the paper.

I already had my hands full with all of the family that was living with me, and I was working twenty-four seven, taking care of all the very elderly women, because God had given me this home. And God was my husband, so joyfully, I got to be at home, and finish raising my Baby Rachelle.

I did not care how many hours I needed to work, also, I got to be at home for my daughter, Mary Michelle, who was my right hand in taking care of this home and helping me, and, faithfully, I was right in the middle of helping her with the same blessings that God was giving to me. So both of my daughters helped me with anything at all that I needed, and I did not have to ask them to help me.

I took for granted that the man and his wife were old, because the ad placed in this newspaper, stated that his wife was in a nursing home. I was too busy to give it any thought, and that God might be expanding my territory, again, because I was only thinking about people who needed nursing help, as I called the number in this ad on the newspaper, but nobody answered. So I left a message that he could call me, if he was interested in having his wife come to my home.

Although, he wanted somebody to be in their home to take care of his wife, so she could get out of the nursing facility, he set up an appointment with me to come over to my home. So, with God's direction in my ministry of providing nursing care to women in need, I thought, maybe, this man would decide to let his wife be in my home.

Also, I thought that God could be expanding my territory, to use me for more of His ministry. Maybe, God wanted me to share some nursing supplies with this man's wife, and, maybe, God wanted me to provide meals for this woman to help her get to go home from that nursing home in Champaign. Her husband said his name was John Reed, and he would bring his son along when he came to the appointment that was agreed upon.

I wanted God to be in complete control of whatever would end up happening, so I placed both of my hands on God's Holy Words and I prayed.

Then at that moment, *I knew that I knew something*, but I was not sure of what I knew, and I only knew that I knew something, and it had to do with my children. So I had Mary Michelle and Rachelle join hands with me, and I led in prayer.

"God, You are in control of our lives, and this is the home that You have given to us, and we thank You, Lord Jesus, for all of these wonderful blessings that are from You. And I know, that I know, that You, Oh Lord

our God, have new a thing for our family. And I know that we are in Your Will for our lives, so whatever You have for us, we will do with Your Blessings, and thank You, Lord Jesus".

19—Dead

◇◇

Then the appointment with John Reed and his son, Grant, came for us to talk about John's wife, Georgia, and a decision was made that he would let his wife stay in my home, because he wanted to get her out of the nursing home in Champaign. Then my son, Mike, came to visit us, because he had not come to see us for several weeks, so all of my children got to meet Grant and his dad that same day.

I was looking forward to sharing all of the blessings that God was doing for my family with this man's wife. Since his wife was in a nursing home, and they needed to have somebody come into their home and take care of her, I thought that meant that they, no doubt, did not have enough money to afford to let her stay with someone. I thought that probably meant they might not have had a nice home and things.

John was not old, so I thought he probably had a real lot of doctor bills and other bills that he was behind on. And he was talking about how his wife had been in the hospital on different occasions, and she had cerebral angiomas that hemorrhaged causing strokes.

My family was made up of very old ladies that I took care of in this big beautiful home that God gave to my children and me, and they shared in the blessings from God. And I prayed for all of them and my children and myself every day and night, and I prayed that God would heal this man's wife, Georgia.

My territory was expanding, as I took care of Georgia, and there were blessings from God, as I listened and blessed others who came to see her. Also, blessings came through getting to minister to hospice nurses who came to over-see her care, and that provided her medical needs.

Grant loved his mom very much, and I prayed that God would heal her, so there were prayer chains going on in different churches, and homes for God to heal Georgia. Of course, John and Grant came to see Georgia daily, and she had company every day.

Georgia shared a bedroom with another lady that was in my home who was a very elderly lady, and her daughter was visiting the morning of May 26, 1998. The usual routine of the hospice nurse that came every day had come, and we gave Georgia her bath, washed her hair, and changed her bedding.

Although, both of these nurses always looked doubtful that Georgia would get well, I knew a Big God was in control of Georgia. And I prayed and quoted healing scriptures to Georgia every day and night. Georgia, just, had to get well for her son, Grant, and that would also make her husband happy.

A couple of nights before Georgia died, I was in the kitchen lying on the couch, because I gave up my bed and every room in my new home, to complete strangers, as unto The Lord. Consequently, I did not have a bed to sleep in, and I did not have an hour for myself, because I was always aware of the needs of my family, and Georgia was part of my family because she lived with me. So a couple of nights before Georgia died, I had fallen asleep, but I was suddenly awakened, because I had never heard Georgia talk, but now, I could hear her saying something. So I quickly ran to her room and stood next to her bed, and I was truly, very excited, because Georgia Reed was looking up toward Heaven, and she seemed to be in control of her eyes, even though, a lot of times, her eyes would go towards her forehead.

However, this night Georgia was looking up toward Heaven, and Georgia Reed was saying in a deep, clear voice, "Thank You, Jesus, thank You, Jesus".

I stood next to this wonderful lady that was praising Jesus, and I did not say a word, because I was so happy to hear her talking to Jesus that I thought Georgia was healed. Then after she stopped praising Jesus, I held her hand, and Georgia closed her eyes, and she did not say another word. I thought she was asleep, so I tucked the blankets under her arms.

Although, I did not call her husband or her son, Grant, I did glance at the clock that was on the dresser in her room, and it was after 3:00 am. I remembered that less than two hours earlier, Grant had just left from helping Mary Michelle and I change his mom's clothes, because I had called him to come and help us.

Grant was very good at helping with his mom any time he could, and he would be over the next day, as usual. His dad had to be out of town on business for his job that night, so that was why I called Grant to come over, and help us with his mom. I never had to call Georgia's husband, because his wife never threw up that much, while she was in my home, and her husband always came to see his wife, and help with her care.

Now, here it was May 26, 1998, and the hospice nurses just left, and the elderly lady's daughter was in the room with her mother and me. Then, as I usually did, I took the elder lady's vital signs, and I wiped off the stethoscope with alcohol and put it in my pocket. Georgia had her own stethoscope and blood pressure monitor, so I was checking her vital signs with them.

However, I could not hear anything with Georgia's stethoscope, and Georgia was looking into my eyes, so I said, "Georgia, I cannot hear your heart, so I'm going to use my stethoscope, because I just used it, and it worked fine".

I laid Georgia's stethoscope on the side of her hospital bed, and reached for her pulse to check it, before I took my stethoscope out of my pocket. At the same time, the elderly lady and her daughter were next to Georgia's bed watching me, and the elderly lady said, "Look at George, she's watching you, Honey".

I was also looking at Georgia, as she had turned her head towards me, and her eyes were looking into my face. Then Georgia surprised me, because she moved her left hand over to my hands, as I was holding her right hand trying to find her pulse. Then Georgia put her left hand on top of my hands, for the first time that I had been taking care of her, but I could still not found her pulse.

I was trying to find Georgia's pulse on her right wrist, like I always felt several times a day, ever since, she had been at my home. However, because Georgia was now holding both of my hands with her left hand, while I was holding her right wrist with both of my hands, I glanced up at her.

Georgia was looking into my face, and a big smile came over her mouth, and she died! Her hand that had come over on top of my hands, fell on top of my hands, and then the telephone started ringing that was right next to Georgia's hospital bed. The elderly lady's daughter pushed the speaker button, and I heard Georgia's husband's voice, and at the same time, I was grabbing my stethoscope out of my pocket.

I was fumbling with my stethoscope, as I was trying to put it on Georgia's chest, over her heart, and her husband was saying, "What's wrong, Mary?"

I cried, "I don't know, because I can't find Georgia's pulse!", and, I had my stethoscope against Georgia's heart, but I could not hear anything, and it was so sad, because Georgia was supposed to get healed!

Why, didn't God heal her? Grant needed his mommy, and Mr. Reed needed Georgia!

Why, didn't God heal Georgia? Everybody wanted Georgia to be healed!

Georgia was going to be the miracle that everybody needed to see, so they would know that Jesus still does miracles today. It was so sad, because Georgia needed to be healed, not dead! It was one of the saddest days of our lives, and poor little Grant, he needed his mommy, as badly as, his daddy needed his wife.

To this very day, every time I think about the day when Georgia died, it tears my heart right out of me. It is so very hard for me to write about it, that I cry and cry, because I wish Grant's mommy was here, so very much, and I would give anything to have her here, instead of me.

I truly love my son, Mike, and my little girls, Mary Michelle and Mary Rachelle, and I thank God for letting me borrow them for the time that I have on this earth. However, God has given me this opportunity, to somehow, get to be another mommy for Grant.

Although, I will never compare to Grant's own mommy, and I will never try to take her place, but I hold up my little boy, and Georgia's little boy in prayer, every day and night.

And when I get to Heaven, I will hug Grant's mom, and tell her how blessed I was to have gotten the golden opportunity to, somehow, try to be part of Grant's life. In that, I ended up marrying his daddy, and I certainly never planned that, because God totally had that planned out, not me.

Georgia Reed was only 55 years old and she has two sons, John and Grant, and her husband that she left behind is John Reed. Georgia was born to Ruth Irene Ketchum York, and Eugene York in Greencastle, Indiana, on September 19, 1942. Georgia had a Bachelor's of Arts Degree in foreign language education, and a Masters Degree in Educational Administration, and Georgia taught school at Danville High School, and Danville Area Community College, and North Ridge Middle School. Georgia went on permanent disability in 1988, because she was paralyzed from cerebral angioma hemorrhages. Georgia and her husband were active members of the Ridgeview Baptist Church in Danville, Illinois.

The cemetery where the burial took place was in Sunset Memorial, and two plots were already chosen and paid for by Georgia and John. The stones that mark the plots have these words on them:

John 3:16
Cogitate Copiously
Matthew 10:22
My Yoke is Easy and
My Burden is Light

Mary went with me to Georgia's visitation that was at Sunset Funeral Home in Danville, while Rachelle and a lady friend stayed with my extended family that was in our home. Then Rachelle and my friend stayed with my extended family, when Mary went with me to the funeral that was at Ridgeview Baptist Church. We were invited to go over to the home where people were going to gather after the funeral, but we needed to get back to our family.

The next day, Mr. Reed and his son, Grant, came to our home and got Georgia's dresser and things, and a man was sent to our home from the hospice office, to pick up her hospital bed and oxygen and tube feeding equipment.

Although, Georgia's husband did not ask for any money back from the monthly payments for taking care of his wife, I was prepared to give him all of the money he had paid me, because I was sure he could use it to help pay for Georgia's medical bills. I told Georgia's husband and son that they were welcome to come and visit, and get anything that might be left in my home from Georgia.

Everything I ever had belonged to God, and I belonged to God and my children belonged to God, and when my husband was alive he belonged to God. We dedicated our children back to God after they were born, because we knew our children were gifts that were borrowed from God, and we were very thankful to God for trusting us with such precious little babies.

We thanked God for everything, and first of all, we gave of our lives into the ministry right after we were married, because we moved two states away where we did not know anybody. And we spent most of our married life teaching and helping people come to know The Lord Jesus Christ, as their own personal Savior. We taught them about tithing to God, although, somehow, I regret to say, our son, Mike, missed that part of our teaching.

The thing about tithing is, first of all, everything belongs to God, because God created everything. God created people, and that means you and me. God created this earth and all of the things that are in it, and God gives people the wisdom, and means to make things from the things that He already made.

You see, God owns people, because God created man and woman, and God created man and woman to reproduce, and, since God created everything, God owns one hundred percent of everything.

If you believe in God, you believe that God owns one hundred percent of everything, and in "The Holy Bible" it says in Leviticus 27:30, "and all the tithe of the land, whether of the seed of the land, or of the fruit of the tree, is the Lord's, it is Holy unto the Lord God.

Tithe means one-tenth, and God owns one hundred percent of everything, including, all of the people on this earth.

God gives people one hundred percent of whatever it is that they have the wisdom, and means to get. God only expects people to give ten percent back to Him, and in "The Holy Bible" God says in Malachi 3: 8-12, it says, "Will a man rob God? Yet you have robbed Me, but you say in what way have we robbed You, in tithes and offerings. You are cursed with a curse, for you have robbed Me even this whole nation.

Bring all the tithes into the storehouse, that there may be food in My house, and try Me now in this, says the Lord of Hosts, if I will not open for you the windows of Heaven and pour out for you such blessing that there will not be room enough to receive it. And I will rebuke the devourer for your sakes, so that he will not destroy the fruit of your ground, nor shall the vine fail to bear fruit for you in the field," Says the Lord of Hosts; And all nations will call you blessed, for you will be a delightful land," Says the Lord of Hosts.

Hebrews 7:8 says, "And here men that die receive tithes; but there He receiveth them, of whom it is witnessed that He liveth.", and Jesus said in John 14:6, "I am the way, the truth, and the life. No one comes to the Father Except through Me!

Then in I Corinthians 2:9 it says,
> But as it is written "Eye has not seen, nor ear heard, nor have entered into the heart of man the things, which God has prepared for those who love Him.", and in I Corinthians 3: 16-17, it says, Do you not know that you are the temple of God, and that the Spirit of God dwells in you?

If anyone defiles the temple of God, God will destroy him. For the temple of God is holy, which temple you are.

God set the example of giving of His best gift to people in John 3: 16, "For God so loved the world that He gave His only begotten Son, that whosoever believeth in Him, Shall not perish but have everlasting life!"

My husband and I could never out-give The Lord, and we gave of ourselves first, and we gave our tithes and offerings that belonged to God.

We did not give this because we expected so many wonderful blessings from God, but we gave to God because God owns everything that we ever had and get and that includes, of course, our children. And we were always so very thankful to God for His many wonderful blessings, and especially our children.

After my husband, Michael, died I continued to belong to God, and everything I ever got belonged to God. Oh, how, I thank God every day and night for His blessings.

After my husband died, I took my Lord and Savior as my Husband, because in "The Holy Bible" it says that God will be a Husband to the widow.

Then God blessed me very much, and everything I prospered in was from God, because God was and is the head of my house and God owns everything I have. And I gave back to God, everything that already belongs to Him, and I have always been glad.

One of the blessings that God gave to me was that I got to take care of Georgia, and I got to meet her family and friends. Then not long after Georgia Reed died, her husband called and asked if he could come over, and I thought Mr. Reed wanted to look at the place where his wife died. Also, I thought Mr. Reed wanted me to give him the remaining part of the money that he deserved to get back from paying me in advance, for taking care of his wife before she died. I was going to give him all of the money back, that he paid me to take care of his wife because I thought he needed it.

When Mr. Reed called me, and asked if he could come over, I remembered something that might be nice. Well, I asked him if he had any videos of his wife that I could watch, so it would help me see what kind of a lady she was when she was not sick. He said he would bring some videos of Georgia and him, and he would watch them with me, and I thought that was kind of him.

I never thought any more about the phone call; because I was very busy taking care of my extended family of elderly women. And I was getting ready to let other ladies that needed my care, come and live in my home.

However, Mr. Reed came to my home before more families were going to move their grandmothers into my home, and he put one of the videos on, and Georgia was talking. Mr. Reed was sitting on one side of my white, leather, sectional couch, and I was sitting on the other end of the couch, so I glanced at him, and realized that he was undoubtedly very sad, because his wife died only a few weeks before then.

I asked Mr. Reed if he would rather that we would not watch the video of his wife, and he said it would be nice to watch it, because he wanted to see the video with Georgia in it. However, I thought, dumb me, most of the time, it would be better that I don't think at all, or, at least, I should keep my mouth shut, because he looked sad.

So, I asked Mr. Reed if he would like for me to sit next to him, while we watched this video. And then before I knew it, Georgia's husband put his arm around me and kissed me. I would never have allowed any man to kiss me on my lips that was married, but his wife died, and my husband had died five years before that.

And, maybe, I should have pushed Mr. Reed away, or, maybe, I should have gotten up real fast and left the room, but I didn't. Instead, dummy me, I fell in love with him that night, and I think we both loved each other that night when we kissed, because he called me and wanted to come back.

I was still working twenty-four seven, taking care of the elderly women that were living with me. And when I got the chance to sleep, I slept on the couch because I gave up all of the bedrooms. Except for the two bedrooms that my two daughters, Mary Michelle and Rachelle, used during the entire time that I had the business of taking care of the women, who lived with my daughters and I, because it was the only way I could take care of that many women.

So, I got very little sleep, and, although I truly liked taking care of the women, I was worn out. I did not know if it was due to all of the company and family that came to see the women, or because all but one of the women had Alzheimer's. The woman that did not have Alzheimer's, had both of her legs from above her knees amputated, before she came to live with us, and all of these women were in need of my full attention, and God gave me the strength, wisdom, and protection that I had to have for this job. Also, Mary was in her early twenties, and Rachelle just turned sixteen, and they were both helping me take care of things to do with my job.

My son, Mike, did not realize John was coming over after his wife died. And I did not include John, in any of my decisions about how I ran my life and business affairs, yet, because we were not going out on dates. So, I told Mike that it would be good, if he would help me find a nice car for Rachelle, because she got me to look at a car that one of her friends grandfathers wanted to sell, and it was not a good deal. So

Mike saw a blue car that he knew was good, and then when I saw that Rachelle liked it, I surprised my daughter, and bought it for her.

The same day that I made the decision to buy the blue car for Rachelle, I got a white Cadillac, because I did not know John Reed and I were going to get married, and I was still doing my business in my home.

In order to get to go someplace to take care of my affairs, like, when I got my taxes done every quarter, Mary Michelle and Rachelle, and most of the time Tina, a lady whose mother lived with us, would stay and sit with the women that I took care of. However, when I went someplace to buy something, I took either Mary Michelle, or Rachelle with me to help me make decisions, because it was always very important to me that all of my children were happy, and that gave me special time alone with one of them.

So, one evening, when John asked me if I would like to go someplace with him, I took Rachelle with me on our first date, and we went for a boat ride. I thought John was totally in debt, because I had never known anybody that had a big beautiful boat with leather seats, and I had never been in a boat so fancy like this one, in all of my life.

I would have to find out from this man that I was falling in love with just how much debt he had, and maybe somehow, we could come to an agreement about how we could help him manage his money, and pay off all of his bills. Although this boat ride was fun, I could not truly enjoy it because I thought John was so foolish to get himself in debt so much, because I asked him whose boat this was, and he said, "Mine".

After that first date, I watched for the right timing when I could address John's bills with him. And I started making decisions about making more money, so I could not only help my daughter pay off her college bills, also, I could help John pay off his bills.

I wished I had not fallen in love with John, because I was afraid he was not a good steward with his money, because I could see that his boat was brand new. I thought maybe he borrowed money to buy it to make some impression on me. Because other men had done foolish things like that when they borrowed money, and got brand new trucks, and houses that they wanted me to see, in order to try to impress me, so that maybe I would go out with them. Also, they made it very clear to me that they wanted me to marry them, and I knew that they would have me paying for all of their expensive toys.

However, I did feel sorry for John, because his wife died, and I hated it because she died in my home. I wished Georgia had never been in our home, because she did not get well like I thought she would. Well, I would counsel with John when the right opportunity presented itself, that he needed to get his bills paid.

I still loved John, and I had told him so, and I would not break his heart by telling him not to come over anymore, because that would make me feel like a real bad person, and I was sure John was a good man. And I was too tired to think straight, what with him coming over to my home, and all of the work and business that I was doing.

I thought about the new truck he drove over to our home after his wife died. Oh, no, I thought, John went out and got a new boat and a new truck, and who knows what else, John may have gone into debt for. He should have been focusing on paying off the doctor and hospital bills, and any other bills that accumulated over the years.

I had to get to the bottom of John's problems before he got further in debt. No telling what other kind of problems he might have. Why was I such a fool as to love a complete stranger? Because the first time I ever met him, was when he brought his son, Grant, to my home for the interview about rather Georgia could be here.

However, at that time I was busy working and taking care of my taxes and other business. Although we talked when his wife was in my home, I really did not know enough about John, and I certainly did not plan on falling in love with him.

It takes years to know somebody well enough to trust him to be the father of your children, and to be your husband. Well, I would not marry John, and I would not let him come back over to my home, until I got his bills straightened out for him.

Then, once, when John and his son, Grant, came to my home, they were upset with business in the church where they were members, because it was being discussed that the church was going to get a music director. John was saying the church could not afford, and did not need another person on staff that needed to be paid a salary, and they were outside on the deck, and the windows were open, so we could hear what they were talking about from inside the house.

It dawned on me that John Reed was a member of the Ridgeview Baptist Church, and I had always gone to Pentecostal churches. Most people in the Pentecostal churches that I had gone to insisted that Baptists were not going to Heaven, because they believed in once saved always saved. The Pentecostals that I knew believed a person will go to Hell for one sin that he commits, so people felt like they needed to confess their sins to Jesus, several times a day.

The Pentecostal beliefs that I was taught was that if you have one sin in your life that is not confessed to Jesus, you have to ask Jesus to take that sin away, and come back into your life. Because you will go to Hell Fire and Brimstone, if Jesus comes back before you get saved, all over again. Also, when you committed one sin, you were guilty of all sins, because when you broke one commandment you were guilty of breaking all of the commandments. So there was a huge difference in the beliefs of the Pentecostals that I knew and Baptists.

So I was doing a real bad thing, because of all the people in the whole wide world, my husband and my dad had both been Pentecostal preachers. I knew better than to ever marry outside of our denomination. Shame on me, what kind of example was I setting for my children, family, friends and all the church people that ever knew me?

20—911

◇◇◇◇◇◇◇◇◇◇◇◇◇◇◇◇◇◇◇◇◇◇◇◇◇◇◇◇◇◇◇◇◇◇◇◇◇◇◇

I went to God in prayer and asked for advice. Also, I searched "The Holy Bible" for myself, for I believed in The Lord Jesus Christ, and I believed that Jesus is God's only Begotten Son, that Jesus was crucified to take away our sins. All we have to do is ask Jesus to take our sins away, and to come into our heart and life.

Then after I ask Jesus to take my sins away, and to come into my heart and life, the only thing I have to do is believe, and have faith in God, that Jesus has taken all of my sins away and come into my heart and life.

Then of course, I want to thank Jesus for being so good to me, that all of my sins are gone, because Jesus has taken all of my sins away, and that means I get to be in heaven with Jesus when I die.

I once was a sinner, but now I am forgiven, and I am on my way to heaven, which means I do not live in fear, of what the future holds. I have all faith in God that God sent His Only Begotten Son into the world, to teach everybody how to live for God, after we are saved.

God counted it righteousness to Abraham that Abraham had such faith, and that is the faith that I have in God, that Abraham did not question God. Abraham did what God told him to do, and God did not send his Son into the world to condemn the world, but God sent His Only Begotten Son into the world to save the world, and Jesus was the only one who, ever, lived in this world that could, possibly, be perfect.

So, no matter, who tells anybody that once you are saved, and forgiven by the blood of the Lord Jesus Christ, that they will go to Hell fire and brimstone for committing one sin, they need to go back to "The Holy Bible" and read what Jesus said in "The Holy Bible" in

John 3:16. Jesus says, "For God so loved the world that He gave His only begotten Son That whosoever believeth in Him Shall not perish, but have everlasting life."

Then after you ask Jesus to take your sins away, and come into your heart and life, the Holy Spirit enters into your heart, because you are forgiven, and all of your sins are gone, and the Lord Jesus Christ lives inside of you.

The Holy Spirit causes you to realize, sin, is sin when you do it, and the Holy Spirit draws you to want to turn away from any sin that you do, and the Holy Spirit causes you to hate sin when you do it. The Holy Spirit is the third part of the trinity of God, and the trinity is God the Father, the Lord Jesus Christ, and the Holy Spirit, and The Holy Spirit causes you to want to draw closer to God.

I want to know God, and the way to know God is to read "The Holy Bible", and pray to Jesus, in "The Holy Bible" in John 14:6 Jesus says, "I am the Way, the Truth, and the Life. No one comes to the Father, except through Me" *Jesus.*

I beg you, please, do not put yourself in torment that you will go to Hell Fire and Brimstone for doing a sin, after you have been forgiven by the Lord Jesus, and asked Jesus to come into your heart and life. For, my whole life through, I have lived in such torment and discouragement, because I did not have the faith in God, to take him at his words.

I could never stop asking Jesus to take my sins away and to come back into my heart and life, because I knew that I was not perfect enough for anybody, and I could never be perfect, so I always worry about going to Hell fire and brimstone.

I put my faith in God, and take Him at his words. For, I have been trying hard, and searching the scriptures, to find out answers for myself, and I have been praying many times a day and night, that God will take all of my fears away, because I do not want to live in fear.

I want the faith that I know, that I know I am on my way to Heaven, because I do not have to fear, I only need to believe, and I do believe, and believe that Jesus has taken all of my sins away, and come into my heart and life once and for all.

194

However, do not be deceived by the enemy sin, because when you or I sin, and the Holy Spirit convicts you and me, we need to repent of that sin before it is too late. Do not sin and think that you will get by with it, because sin always finds you out, and everything that is hidden will come out into the open.

Jesus Christ conquered the enemy sin at Calvary, and that makes it easy for you and me to ask Jesus to forgive us when we deliberately sin.

However, keep in mind that after you have confessed your sins to Jesus and asked Him to forgive you and come into your heart and life, the Holy Spirit will convict you of your desires to sin, and the Holy Spirit will help you surrender your life completely to the Lord Jesus Christ.

Talk to Jesus and pray for Jesus to help you, because Jesus will not turn you away, Jesus is right here with you all of the time and he loves you more than anybody can ever love you.

God will not be mocked, so do not think you will get into heaven with sin in your life. Try not to sin, but when you do sin, repent before it is too late for you, because you do not know when you will die. Do you want to go to Hell when you die, no you do not, you want to go to Heaven when you die, so do not sin, because all sin is against God, and God does not tolerate any kind of sin.

You should be afraid, if you are sinning, however, if you have asked Jesus to take your sins away when you sin, and you truly repent of your sins, and ask Jesus to come into your heart and life, He forgives you and stays right there in your heart, and you are on your way to Heaven when you die, and you and I will, for sure, die!

Jesus went to Calvary and was crucified once and for all, to take away the sins of everybody in the world that asks Him to. And Jesus never has to go back to Calvary, because He already arose to take us to Heaven when we belong to him. So never ask Jesus to do what He has already done for you and me, because He already did it.

Jesus was already crucified for you and me, and everybody else that accepts Jesus, and He already took all of my sins away and came into my heart and life to stay. Now, all I have to do is to live for Jesus, and that is why I want to read and study "The Holy Bible" for myself, because I want to know about God and Jesus and the Holy Spirit, and how to live for Jesus.

Now, give God all the praise and glory that is so very much due Him, Hallelujah, and do not live in fear, but conquer the enemy of fear in your life and live for Jesus.

Do not live in fear, for once you have asked the Lord Jesus Christ to take all of your sins away and come into your heart and life, believe that Jesus has taken your sins away and come into your heart and life. Then follow the Holy Spirit's leading, and do not let sin come between you and God, and do not sin, because all sin is against God. The Holy Spirit will help you know what sin is, and The Holy Spirit will help you read and understand "The Holy Bible", so you will know what God has taught people and what God has to teach you.

One evening, John came over to my home, and I asked him to tell me about his debts, because he already knew that my home was paid for. I had the deed to my home proudly displayed on the wall in a picture frame, since last winter, and it showed that my home was paid for.

However, I had taken a lean out on my home to help my daughter, Mary Michelle, pay for college bills. I wanted John to know that I was going to continue to help my daughter, because she had been helping me raise Rachelle, ever since, their daddy died five years earlier. Also, Mary had been helping me take care of my business and home.

John smiled and said, "What debt".

John asked me to marry him not long after that, and he wanted to get married in a couple of months. However, we both had to take care of our own business that had to do with making sure taxes did not get screwed up. Also, I needed to make room for John in my home, because I still had women living with me that I took care of. Then I also had unfinished business to take care of with families that wanted their parents that had Alzheimer's to live with me. So we would take care of our own affairs over the next couple of months, then we would get married the first of the year.

John could take all of his and Georgia's tax affairs for the entire year of 1998, and I could take care of my business affairs and taxes for that year. Also, I would not take any more people into my home, because I would need to have time to take care of our marriage.

Then, John and I would need to have a bedroom, because I had given up my bedroom to complete strangers as unto the Lord. For I believed "The Holy Bible" taught that when you let somebody come into your home and live with you, and eat your food, and take care of them it is doing that for Jesus. Even though, I got paid for my services, I did it knowing that God was always watching everything I did, and God is the husband to the widow, and a husband provides for his family.

God paid for everything and helped me with the business in my home, although I worked very hard and so did my children. I had planned on giving everything I had to my three children when God took me to Heaven.

I was hoping my daughters would live in our home, and it would be their homestead, for the rest of their lives. So, I had put my hands in the cement sidewalks and driveway before it dried, also, I had written dates and love notes in the cement.

Well, it was on January 1, 1999, when President Bill Clinton was in office, and the European Economic Community established the Euro as their common currency. And Illinois got sixteen inches of snow, with drifts as high as eight feet in front of the church where John and I were getting married, and the temperatures were well below zero degrees Fahrenheit.

The weather did not keep us from getting married, on January 2, because we were in love, and my beautiful sister, Miriam, and a lot of her family came a long way to our wedding.

John's sister, Linda, and her husband, Mike, and their sons, Clay and Drew, and John's mom, Irene, who was escorted by Drew, and my precious mom, Flossie, who was escorted by my brother, Jim, all participated in our wedding.

My son, Mike, escorted me and gave me away during the ceremony. My daughters, Mary Michelle and Mary Rachelle, were my maids of honors, and a close friend of ours, Jack, and John's son, Grant, stood up with John.

The cutest little girl in the world, Brittany, was our flower girl, and my sister, Miriam's, grandson, Jason, was our little ring bearer.

John and I traveled and we got to go places like out west, and I got to see my favorite pastor and his wife, and my favorite singing group, Treasure, a singing group that includes my niece and her husband, Lori and Jim, and their son and a beautiful friend, Joy, as they sang unto The Lord.

Then in the fall of 2001, we got a chance to go on a vacation in Wyoming, also, we went to Yellowstone National Park and saw Old Faithful (**See Book Cover**), which is a fairly big geyser that goes off about once every hour. And there are geysers all over the ground around different areas that were bubbling and steaming, so people could not just let their children or pets take off running. Because there were signs all around those places that warned people to be aware of those places that are hazards, and then we went on to Glacier National Park up into the Glacier Mountains in Montana.

On the night of September 10, 2001, John and I stayed in Kalispell, Montana. In the morning, about 7:00 (9:00 Eastern), on September 11, 2001, terrorists in jet planes attacked the twin towers in New York City, New York. John was watching it as it was happening on television, as I was finishing my shower when he told me to sit down, and watch what was happening on television.

We were in shock, and so was everybody else, and we prayed for God to protect our country. President Bush was on television after that, and declared that he would get those terrorists that caused this to happen to us, and our military went to war with them.

People all over the United States just wanted to be with their families, so, of course, we started our journey back home to be with our children.

On September 11, 2001, Rachelle was buying a nice home in Danville where she lived, after I found a buyer for her so she could sell her mobile home. Then on December 8, 2001, she had a banquet in her home in honor of Mary Michelle who graduated with a Bachelor of Science Degree in Business.

Mary Michelle graduated from Easter Illinois University, and she got a job with Erie Insurance, in Illinois. Then Mary moved out of our home in Danville, into a nice duplex home in Charleston, Illinois.

At the same time, John and I started doing work around Mom Reed's home to help her, because John's sister, Linda, and her husband,

Mike, were doing almost everything for her. Then it wasn't long before Mom Reed needed to live with Linda and Mike, so John and I would bring Mom Reed to our home for awhile, to give Linda time for things she needed to do.

When Mom wasn't at our home, and John and I caught up on things around our home, we would go fishing. Then we got to have fun riding on the rivers and lakes in our fancy boat.

Sometimes we went to Lake Shelbyville, and we stopped by Mary Michelle's home to visit her. It was always a treat to see my daughter because she was so busy with her job, and the new home that she lived in, and then buying a big new home, that I hardly ever got to see her.

It was only about sixty miles from our home in Danville to Mary Michelle's home in Charleston, but it wasn't very often that I went to see her. I am a homebody, and I do not like to go places by myself.

Most of the time when we got to be with our daughter, it was when she came to Danville to visit us. Although Mary and I called each another as often as we could, it was fun, because sometimes I would go to Mary's home and spend the night with her.

It was fun having a condominium in Sandestin, Florida, and John and I went there for our honeymoon. Then we spent the winters there, after he retired. We did not have to worry about shoveling snow, instead, we got to walk on the white sandy beach, and have fun in the Gulf of Mexico.

Then one winter, after we painted the inside of the condominium, and we got back home in Danville, our condo association called us, and said that the condo had been ruined. A hose from the washer in the upstairs condo came loose, and water had been coming into our condo for several hours. So we went back to Florida, and our partners, Sue and Jim, and John and I agreed on everything that had to be done to the condo, in order make it nice, again.

Then our sons, Grant and Mike, went with us to Florida, and helped us bring back all of the furniture from the condo that was going to be thrown out, because it had all new furnishings. Mike made a nice trailer that we took with us, which we piled high with the furniture, and we really looked like "rednecks" as we drove back home all the way from Sandestin to Danville. However, it wasn't long before our partners, and we got a chance to sell the condominium and make a profit.

I had been praying that my son, Mike, would be blessed with a lovely young wife that I knew God had for him, someplace. I love Mike very much, and, of course, I wanted him to have the best wife that there is any place in the whole wide world. Then I was talking to my sister, Linda, on the phone one day and she made arrangements for me to have Mike call a friend of hers, Stacy Jo, so I gave my son Stacy Jo's phone number.

Mike and I were preparing to make chili for some place that he promised to bring it, also, he was helping John put in a circle, paved drive-way at our home. I kept telling Mike to call Stacy Jo, and he said after he got a shower, he would call her.

I said, "Mike, I'll make your chili for you, if you will call this young lady that Aunt Linda set up an appointment with for you. Mike, you can even use my phone to call her, because Stacy Jo might be expecting you to call her, because you told me to let Aunt Linda know that you would talk to Stacy Jo on a certain day, at a certain time".

It may not have seemed like it, but I wanted my son, Mike, to marry Stacy Jo. I knew my son would fall in love with Stacy Jo, as soon as, he laid eyes on her. Because I was praying for Mike and Stacy Jo, and I knew, that I knew that Mike would take one look at Stacy Jo, and fall in love with her. And he did, and I was so glad, and I am still so glad that Mike fell in love with Stacy Jo.

Mike and Stacy Jo got married on January 4, 2003, and their wedding was beautiful. Stacy Jo was so precious that she let her best friend, who is my sister, Linda, and her husband, Mike's daughter, Sara, be her maid-of honor, and my daughters, Mary and Rachelle, be her bride's maids.

Stacy Jo's daddy, Bob, gave her away. And Stacy Jo looked so beautiful to me, as she walked down the isle of the First Baptist Church, in Danville, Illinois. Her mommy, Kathy, and I lit a unity candle together. And I wanted to tell Kathy how much I wished, and still would love, to be close friends with her, because we became one family, when we lit that candle together.

Just forget about hurt feelings, and, as my son, Mike, said to me one time, "Don't go there". Let us not go there to past hurt feelings, and things that keep us from spending time together, that we can never get back.

Life is too short for any of us not to take advantage of what time we have here on this earth, because we need to be real good friends and one family, together, the way God intended for us to be. I love Kathy and Stacy Jo, and I always want them to be part of my life, and for us to have fun together.

After Stacy Jo and my son, Mike, got married they lived in Mike's condominium in Danville, until, he got his job transfer to Southern Illinois, which is where Stacy Jo's family and parents have their church that they minister in.

Mike and Stacy Jo bought a home in Illinois, and fixed it up the way they wanted it to be. Then they became the proud parents of Samuel Isaiah, born on January 14, 2004, which is close to Stacy Jo's birthday on January 1. Then they became the proud parents of Elijah Michael, born on July 23, 2005, and then they became the proud parents of Hannah Elizabeth, born on December 14, 2006. Also, Stacy Jo and Mike, as well as, Cindy and Grant, have babies who are in Heaven, because Jesus took them before they developed to full term.

In 2003, our son, Grant, was living close to Chicago, Illinois, when Cindy came into his life. And, boy's oh boy, were we ever blessed to have Cindy come into Grant's life, because Grant not only fell in love with this remarkable young Christian lady, I did too. Well, I mean, I didn't fall in love with Cindy, but I really do love her, and she is very precious to all of us.

On November 1, 2003, Grant married this Christian lady, Cindy, and her mommy, Sunny, and I have been best friends, also, her daddy, Larry, is John and my best friend. Her family lives close to Columbus, Ohio, and that was where Cindy and Grant wanted to live, because they both had jobs in Ohio.

Cindy and Grant lived in an apartment, until they decided to buy a house, and then we helped them move to their new home in Ohio, and they lived happily ever after. Then Cindy and Grant became the proud parents of their son, Isaac Levi, born on July 21, 2006, and Caleb Ethan, born on February 13, 2012.

In 2004, Rachelle moved up in her career, so we moved Rachelle out of the home that she was buying in Danville, to a home in Toledo, Ohio, where she worked, until, she was promoted to another job in Center Line, Michigan. Rachelle got promoted again and again, until she ended up in Jackson Hole, Wyoming, and that really tore me up, because I missed our daughter, Rachelle, so much.

Things were happening, so fast, for Rachelle with her promotions in the job that she had, that John and I did not get to go and see her very often, and we never went to Jackson Hole, Wyoming, at all. I was so worried about Rachelle that I called her a lot, and I prayed every day and night for her, and God answered my prayers.

It broke Mary Michelle's heart when we sold our home in Illinois, because she liked our home so much that she wanted to live there again someday. However, John assured me that I could go and see her anytime I wanted to, and that caused Mary and I to both feel somewhat better.

But I am a homebody, and I do not like to go places by myself. And our daughter was working so much, that she could not possibly come and see us. Well, God is in control of our lives, and God had it all planned out ahead of time.

Mary met a handsome young man, Tim Partlow, and she did not tell us about him. She had moved out of her condominium in 2003, into a beautiful new home that she was buying, and we thought our daughter was, either always working at her job, or spending time working around her new home that she bought in Charleston, Illinois.

Of course, we knew Mary was active in her church, and she spent time with some of her lady friends. But she was keeping Tim Partlow a big secret from us, and, of course, that was okay, because she would tell us when she was ready.

One spring day in 2007, my little Baby Rachelle moved from Jackson Hole, Wyoming, all the way to our home and her home, here in Gallatin, Tennessee. I was so happy, and I am still very glad that I prayed and prayed, thanking my Lord Jesus for answering my prayers, and Rachelle stayed with us, until she got a job in Nashville.

Rachelle moved to a nice condominium close to her job, and we get to see our daughter any time we want to. Rachelle and I have a lot of fun going out together, and we take full advantage of any opportunities that we can, to spend time with each other. Isn't God Good, and God answered my prayers; my precious Rachelle and I are very close; oh, how I thank Jesus for answering my prayers.

Mary's handsome young man was, and is a wonderful man, Tim Partlow, and they fell in love. He came to visit us with our daughter, and we liked him right from the start. Then after they dated for a while, Tim gave Mary an engagement ring, and asked her to marry him, and they made plans for their wedding. Then Mary sold her home in Charleston, and Tim and Mary bought a big home in Effingham, Illinois.

Tim and Mary Michelle got married on August 25, 2007, and their wedding was beautiful. Mary looked like an angel, because she was so beautiful, and Tim was very good looking. Mary asked her sister and best friend, Rachelle, to be her maid-of-honor.

Tim's mom, Susie, and I have been good friends from when we first met, and we lit a unity candle together at Mary and Tim's wedding. Tim's dad, Bill, became John and my good friend, as soon as we met him. So our families are very happy, and we have good times together.

Tim and Mary got pregnant about three years after they were married, making John and I the proud grandparents of Christian Michael, on June 3, 2010. Then a few months later they got pregnant again, and made us the proud grandparents of Trenton Scott, on October 25, 2011, yea, and John and I are so very happy to get the blessings of grandchildren.

John said he did not want me to have people live with us that I need to take care of. So I got to focus all of my attention on John and our children. Then I was free to help his sister, Linda, take care of Mom Reed, when John and I were not traveling.

I was real happy that John had such a wonderful mom, and she liked me right from the start. We had several things in common, because her mom died and my mom died when we were both, almost the same ages.

Then a little over ten years after Mom Reed's son and I got married, Mom died, February 23, 2009. John and I, and so many other close family and relatives, got to have the golden opportunity to get to be with Mom before she died.

With sadness of heart, I felt the yearning of going to Heaven, and see Jesus, and Mom Reed, and my husband, Mike, and Georgia, John's late wife. Joy entered my soul, as I thought about, getting to see my parents again, and how magnificent it will be when we see King Jesus on His throne.

Because right, now, what you do counts, forever, after you are dead. Because your soul goes on to live, in whatever choice you make, forever, in eternity.

Isaiah 40:31 says:
    But those who wait on the Lord
    Shall renew their strength,
    They shall mount up with wings like eagles,
    They shall run and not be weary,
    They shall walk and not faint.

Psalms 42:1 says:
    As the deer pants for the water brooks,
    So pants my soul for You, O God.
    My soul thirsts for God, for the living God.
    When shall I come and appear before God?

Joshua 24:15 says:
    And if it seems evil to you to serve the Lord,
    Choose for yourselves this day, whom you will serve,
    But as for me and my house,
    We will serve the Lord.

John 8:12 says:
    Then Jesus spoke to them again, saying,
    I am the light of the world.
    He who follows Me shall not walk in darkness,
    But have the light of life.

Jesus Christ and God have adopted you, if Jesus lives inside you right now. The best inheritance that anybody can have is to know, you have been adopted into the Kingdom of God through Christ Jesus.

For God will supply all your needs according to his riches in glory, because God is always looking after you, and God will always take care of His children.

Your life belongs to God, so never worry about tomorrow, because God is in tomorrow and you will truly be taken care of.

You are a child of the only, living God, so Go and live for Christ Jesus!

Conquer the enemy of despair and hurt memories that have enslaved you, way too long.

May you have peace, joy, and love from God. Live as God teaches you to with longsuffering, gentleness, goodness, faith, meekness, and temperance of attitude.

Your attitudes toward hurtful people will destroy you.

Or, you can bear fruits of the spirit as God teaches you. But the greatest of these is to love, as Christ loves you.

Let your hurtful memories and heart, be healed by our Lord Jesus Christ.

Let Christ's love for you saturate your memories with healing, and powerful, loving memories of good things.

Christ has blessings for you, to put in place of those hurtful memories that gives you peace that surpasses all understanding.

You are a child of God, and Jesus is healing your memories, and turning your memories into blessings, right now.

You are a child of God, so go with these thoughts, love, peace, joy, longsuffering, gentleness, goodness, faithfulness, meekness, and temperance of attitude. And try to live the way God wants you to, so blessings will come to you, because you are a very precious child that God has adopted into His fold.

God will take you to Heaven when it is your time to die.

Death is only a doorway, to get to be in Heaven, where peace and blessings await you in Heaven. Jesus loves you so much, and Jesus is waiting for you to come and be with Him in Heaven.

I'm so glad that God does not hold hurtful memories against people. He came into the world to set us free from the slavery of hurtful memories that try to rob us of our fruits of the spirit.

Alleluia Jesu Cristo tee Adoramos. Jesu Cristo te exallamos, I come to You, Lord Jesus, Alleluia Jesu Cristo te Adoramos Jesu Cristo tee exallamos, and I Praise The Lord Most High, thank You, Jesus, which is what I speak in tongues, as The Holy Spirit uses me to praise God.

Hurtful memories were zapping my peace of mind, and freedom and joy and contentment, until I was sick. And I was, almost, conquered for a while by the enemy. Although, I would make a conscious choice to never think about all of the hurtful memories in my mind, the slavery to them for so long would cause me to start thinking about them, again.

Did I want to be conquered by the enemy, again? Not hardly.

But I was hurt, so badly, and some people would hurt me all over, again. And they would tell me that I was a liar, because nobody had ever been mean to me and hurt me, because they thought that everybody was good to me.

Those people were letting the enemy use them to try and conquer my spirit, and it caused me to shed many tears in great anguish. No peace and joy can come from people who cause pain to you, and leave you with hurtful memories. Those kinds of memories are not from God, and that is for sure. So when you wonder if somebody is being used of God, watch for the fruits of the spirit in their lives.

You need to make a conscious effort to put your painful memories into the hands of Jesus, and he will heal you. Do not cause pain in anybody's life, but forgive others for the painful memories they have caused in your life, and set yourself free from bondage that is ruining your life.

Being free from hurtful memories will set you up for God to expand your territory of a sweet attitude. Do not waist your mind and your life any longer, by allowing hurtful memories to enslave you, and to conquer the life right out of you.

Because one of God's blessings for your life is to set you free from everything, at all, that causes you pain and hurtful memories.

Everybody has done something, or, a lot of things that caused pain, and painful memories resulted from the pain of it. Give all of the pain, and painful memories to Jesus Christ, right now, and do not live another day, or even another minute, with all of that pain in your memories.

21—Thoughts to Ponder

It was in March of 2008, and President George W. Bush was in office, when gold hit $1,000 an ounce, and I was sick and dying. I would make myself eat, although, my appetite was almost completely gone. I had an infection that I was taking antibiotics to get rid of, and there was so much pain in my entire body that I needed to take prescription pain killers.

My body was getting weaker every day, and my skin and lips were looking pale blue. My weight was down to only 93 pounds, and it was obvious that I was dying a slow, painful death.

Then a warm feeling came over my entire body, and I knew, somehow, that everything was going to be good from then on. I felt a sense of relief and happiness, as I relaxed in a cloud, of what felt like, was goodness and mercy, because I had no pain. And my body felt limp, as I could feel myself leaving this body that I had been in for so many years.

My husband, John, has his own story to tell about what happened that day in April of 2008, because John said that he was upstairs in his office, and he heard me crying, so he asked me what was wrong, and he said I kept crying.

However, I was lying over the side of the table, with my head next to my plate, and my legs were caught in the arms of the chair that I was sitting on, and I was not moving or crying, by the time he got downstairs.

John said he talked to me, but I did not respond to him, and I was not crying, or talking or responding to anything by the time he got downstairs. And John said he got me out of the chair, and he laid me on the kitchen floor, next to the chair that I was sitting in.

John said he could see that I was not breathing, so he told me to breathe. He could see that I was verily taking a shallow breath, when he was insisting that I breathe, so due to the condition that I was in, he called 911.

John related his story, several times, to people after that, because of course, they wanted to know what happened. John said that a fire truck came, and an ambulance came, within five minutes to our home; for there is a fire station within five miles from our home.

I was put on a gurney, and taken in the ambulance to the hospital, and I don't think I was dead, but the fact is that I am not afraid to die. Actually, I truly look forward to death, because that is the door to Heaven where Jesus is, and all of our loved ones are waiting there for people when they die.

There is no fear in death, oh Death, where is thy sting? I have had so many, fantastic, glimpses of what it will be like, after anybody dies, that has Jesus Christ living in their heart and life, because all of the glimpses, of what it will be like after death are from "The Holy Bible".

Anyone can read God's Words in "The Holy Bible", *and you know, that you know,* that Heaven is a Blessed Grand Place where there are mansions awaiting everyone, and there are streets of purest gold. Read "The Holy Bible" for yourself and all of your fears about dying will turn into excitement. Yes, I am looking forward to dying and being with Jesus, and everybody that is already in Heaven!

I opened my eyes, and wondered where I was, and I could see my husband, John, standing at the end of the room, and he was talking to a person that looked like a nurse. As I looked at John, I could see that he had a sad look on his face, and I wondered, "Is John sad, and what is going on?"

Then I felt cold all over my body, so I said, "I'm cold", and John walked over to me, and then I could see that I was lying on a bed, and John looked grim, as he told me, "You are in the emergency room in the hospital".

I was confused about why I was in the hospital, and I just wanted to go home, and I was cold, so I repeated, "I'm cold".

John told the nurse who was in the room that I was cold, and I needed a blanket, so within a few minutes, I was covered up with a warm blanket. Different things were done to me, as I was checked over, so it could be determined what was wrong with me.

My vital signs were going from one extreme to the other extreme, for the entire time that I was in this emergency room, and a blood pressure cuff was kept on my arm that showed the extremes on a monitor next to the bed. An IV was connected from a machine to my arm with fluids running into my veins.

A doctor came into the room at different times that I had never seen before, and he would look at me as though I was spaced out, when he kept telling me to do different things, like move my hand and foot, and I wondered, "What is wrong with this doctor, can't he see that I am moving my hands and feet?"

However, that same doctor would come back into the room where I was, and tell me to move my hands and feet, again, and I was trying, real hard, because I wanted to go home.

So, I tried to sit up, but the whole right side of my body, did not come with the left side of my body, when I started to move without thinking about rather, or not my body would move. And it felt like there was something wrong, and John was standing next to the bed where I was lying. I just wanted to go home, because I was confused, and I did not know why they were putting me in a room in the hospital.

I went to sleep, and when I woke up I thought I heard an angel talking very quietly, so when I opened my eyes I saw my little daughter, Mary Michelle.

And for just a couple of seconds I thought that I saw an Angel right there next to my baby!

I looked at my daughter, and I may have been imagining it, but I thought there was a light that was next to her, and the light was in the form of a person that could have been an Angel! It was so bright that all I could see was a bright light in the form of a big person next to my baby.

Mary was crying, and saying to me, "Mommy, I love you, so much".

I looked at my little angel, Mary Michelle, which was what I called my little pumpkin, Mary, a lot of times, ever since I imagined, or saw an Angel next to her, a long time ago.

Mary Michelle was with her handsome husband, Tim, in the hospital room with me where I was brought after I was in the emergency room, and somehow, I knew that I was dying, however, I would not tell anybody.

I knew that I would never go home again, and I would get to die and be with Jesus, like I wanted to be for so many years, and the only thing I regretted was that my precious children would miss me.

My youngest daughter, Rachelle, came into the hospital room where I was lying in bed. Then when she stood closer to the bed where I was lying, I may have imagined it, but I thought I saw the same light that was in the form of a big person.

This form was so bright that it looked just like what I was sure was an Angel that I was, either imagining or really was, with little Pumpkin when I first saw her in the room.

Rachelle just shined, as the brightness shown upon her, and I blinked, because I could not keep my eyes open for more than a couple of seconds, and when I looked again I could not see this brightness that I thought might be an Angel anymore.

The brightness of the light was in the form of a big person, and I did not want to miss out on seeing this brightness if it was actually an Angel, because I could no longer see the brightness that was beside Mary Michelle, and I thought.

"This is an Angel that is still with my little Baby Rachelle, and I wonder if she knows it"!

This bright light that was in the form of a big person, had to be an Angel that was with my little Baby Rachelle, and it was just like the light that was with Mary Michelle.

I stared in amazement at the brightness that I thought for sure was an Angel, just long enough that I had to blink, and then I did not see the brightness when I opened my eyes again.

This Angel was in the form of a big tall person that was a bright light that was so close to Rachelle that nothing could have been put between them.

Then I blinked again, and I could not see this Angel, anymore, although, *I knew, that I knew,* that this Angel was still right there, so close to my little Baby Rachelle that I could relax, and die without any worries about my children.

I had seen Angels so close to both of my daughters that I knew Jesus was right beside my daughters taking care of them. And Jesus was always with my little babies taking care of them for me, and I could die in peace, *and, I knew, that I knew,* that I was going to Heaven when I died.

My son, Mike, called and talked to me on John's cell phone, and I told him to come and see me in the hospital.

I would not have told my handsome, young son, Mike, to come and see me in that hospital, but I was sure it would not be long, before I died. And my little, precious son would be hurt, if he did not get to see me, before I died.

When Mike came into the hospital room, I saw that same bright light, which I was sure, was an Angel that was with him!

I was sure that at any moment I would die and be in Heaven with Jesus!

And I stared in such fascinating amazement, at my son who was standing at the end of the bed, with that bright light that I was sure was an Angel, right next to him!

That Angel was just as bright as the ones that I saw when Mary Michelle and Rachelle first came into this room. And I was so glad that Jesus let me see Angels with my children, because *I knew that I knew*, that there are Angels with everybody.

Sometimes, Jesus opens our eyes to see the thrill of some of His Heavenly Angels here on earth with His children, and this is a very significant gift from Jesus to His children.

I saw a very bright light that I was sure was an Angel because it was in the form of a tall person. Although, I only saw the bright light for a moment that was with each and every one of my children, when they were in that hospital room with me, and I knew that I was dying. Even though, I only saw the bright light for just a moment.

However, *I knew that I knew* that Angels were still right there, so close to each and every one of my children that nothing could get between them, because this brightness, in the form of a human being, covered over part of the side of each and every one of them when I saw it.

I did not tell Mike or anybody, that I saw Angels with my children, because I thought for sure, it was my time to get to die. And I thought that, probably, they did not see their Angels, because they would have said so.

So, all of our children came to see me, while I was in the hospital. And I tried, so hard, to move my body to take care of myself, because I could not handle seeing my children so sad. Also, my son, Grant, came to see me, and a lot of our friends came to see me, while I was in the hospital, and I tried real hard to move my extremely, heavy, right arm.

Then when a doctor came into the room where I was, I had to tell him that Jesus is The Savior. And that did not go over well with my husband, John, but I told him that I needed to tell this doctor about Jesus. And that doctor really did not like it that I talked about Jesus, but I needed to tell everybody about Jesus.

There will be some people that will not die, because those are the people that are still alive when The Lord Jesus comes back to earth.

It tells about this in the book of Revelation in "The Holy Bible". After the rapture takes place, the people who realize that they missed out on the rapture will be able to repent and turn to God.

And Jesus will take their sins away when they repent and turn to God, also, Jesus will come into their hearts and lives. And those people that are still on the earth after the rapture will need to keep their life pure, and not take the mark of the beast.

If you are left on this earth, after the rapture of the saints takes place, I beg you do not take the mark of the beast, no matter what the cost.

All of the torture and pain in the whole, wide world is better than to die and go to Hell Fire and Brimstone.

Do not take the mark of the beast, even if it means you and your family and friends have to be tortured and burned, because the mark of the beast means that a person is not a Christian.

Be careful that you do not take the mark of the beast. If, somehow, you get the mark of the beast put on your hand, get rid of that mark. Get the mark of the beast off your body, but do not kill yourself. Please, do not take the mark of the beast.

This is a warning for the end of times.

After the rapture takes place, people will try to force you to take the mark of the beast, but do not let anybody put the mark of the beast on you.

Live for the Lord Jesus Christ and you will be saved. Jesus will take care of you. Do not be deceived by false prophets. Read "The Holy Bible" and ask Jesus to take all of your sins away, and come into your heart and life, and thou shalt be saved.

I am on my way to Heaven to see my Lord Jesus, very soon, and I want to see all of you in Heaven, too, when you die.

Jesus is waiting on the Right side of God, next to the Throne of God, for everybody that is a child of God, to come home to Heaven. And, we are adopted children of God, when Jesus is in our hearts and lives, so Praise, Jesus, forever!

Our children helped John and I with all kinds of important things, which helped ease the burden of both John and I. Tim mowed and trimmed, not only our yard, but also, the lot across the street from our home that John takes care of, plus, Tim did a lot of other kind things that helped at lot.

Mary Michelle and Rachelle got all of the supplies that were needed for me, while I was in this hospital, and Mary Michelle insisted on staying with me every night when her husband and she were here, and she did everything for me that she could to help.

Rachelle came to our home when I was too sick to clean my own home, and she cleaned and worked, until everything was spotless, also she came and sat with me several times, when I was too sick to even know that she was there.

Before our son, Mike, left we prayed, and he asked Jesus to heal his mom, and he kissed me and told me that he had a lot of people praying for me. And I thought, "Oh, my precious Mike, I am not going to get well, because I am going to die, Honey, because it is my time to get to die and be with Jesus in Heaven."

Before Grant left he might have kissed me on the right side of my cheek, but I did not feel it, because I did not feel any of my children kiss me on the right side of my face. However, I sensed that they kissed me good-bye, because I could feel their breath on the left side of my nose when they leaned over me.

I could have lost my son, Grant, and my daughter-in-law, Cindy, in January of 2004, only a few weeks after they were married, and then we would not have our cute, little grandsons, Isaac Levi and Caleb Ethan, which would be an awful disappointment to think about.

It was when Grant had an appointment, and Cindy was going with Grant to Mayo Clinic in Rochester, Minnesota, from where they lived in Ohio, and they were driving a fairly new, white truck, and they had only driven for about an hour when their truck turned, totally, upside down on the icy snowy road. There had been a snowstorm, however, Grant had appointments with doctors at Mayo that he did not want to cancel, because it is hard to get appointments there, when it is convenient for you.

Grant and Cindy both got out of that white truck, when it was upside down in the icy snow, and they were not hurt. Thank You, Lord Jesus, for bringing Grant and Cindy out of that truck without injuries to them.

After they called and let us know what happened, I prayed for Cindy because she had recently been in a car wreck before that. I knew Cindy was probably more stressed out about the accident that happened in the white truck than Grant was, even though, the wreck that Cindy was in caused her not to be able to do some things, she got the golden opportunity to meet my son, and then Cindy and Grant got married on November 1, 2003.

Grant's appointments at Mayo Clinic with the doctors were to check on the status of his genetic, neurological defects, for which, he had previously had three brain surgeries, and he was on medications that were being evaluated by these doctors. Then after all of the tests were done, and the results came back, Grant did not need to take the medicine any longer, because all of the tests indicated that his condition had not further deteriorated.

Grant told us that he did not have to take any more medicine because the results were good, but he was taken in an ambulance to the hospital in 2007. Grant's neurological condition had again deteriorated. So John drove to Ohio, to be with our children, and I was too sick to go, so I prayed for Grant. And a lot of other people prayed for him, too, and then God healed Grant, again.

My children went back to their homes, and I was still in that hospital, and I was not getting better. So plans were made for me to go to a skilled facility, and John brought extra clothes in a suitcase from home, for me to wear at the skilled nursing facility that was expecting me. Then the paper work was in order, and I was ready to go, and John was sitting next to the hospital bed that I was on.

There were people praying for me, and my own children and husband were praying for me. Although, I thought for sure it was my time to get to die, and go to Heaven and be with Jesus, but God is The One in Control. For healing power had already been going throughout my body, and I was awake that night praying.

My husband and I were patiently waiting for the therapist and doctor to come into the hospital room and check on my condition. Then I would be moved to a skilled nursing facility that was close to the hospital, where I would have therapy every day, to try and help me get better. But, it was not God's will for me to be in the nursing facility, because a miracle was going to happen for me, as I felt such warmth and coolness, both at the same time, go all over my body.

The therapist came into the room to check on me, and by then I was sitting in a chair, and I told her, "I'm healed, I am healed because Jesus healed me, and I want to walk because Jesus healed me."

However, the therapist tried to take my arms and help me get up out of the chair, as she insisted, "Let me help you".

I refused to let the therapist help me, and I told her, "No, I want to get up from this chair with the help of Jesus, and I want to walk with the help of Jesus, because Jesus has healed me, and Jesus will help me stand up and walk".

I got up from that chair with the help of Jesus, and Jesus walked with me all the way out of that room, and way down that hallway, in that hospital.

And, I was praising God, and thanking Jesus for healing me with every step that I took, Praise God, because Jesus completely healed me. I am healthier now than I had been in years, ever since Jesus healed me that day in April of 2008, which is over four years ago, right after my Baby Rachelle's birthday, which is on April 11, that Jesus healed me, and I have been thanking Jesus, ever since.

It was May 20, 2008, when we got a phone call that told us my son, Mike, had been riding his motorcycle home from work that evening, and a truck pulled out in front of him, and my son was in critical condition and taken to a hospital.

And I cried out to God, "Lord Jesus, oh, please, don't let Mike die; Jesus, please, heal my son!"

Mike worked at a dangerous job for over fifteen years, and Mike and his wife, Stacy Jo, had already been married for almost five and a half years. And they have three children, Samuel, who was born January 14, 2004, Elijah, who was born July 23, 2005, and Hannah, who was born December 14, 2006.

Yes, God healed my son, Mike, however, it took time, and Mike did everything he was told to do, in order, to help get better as fast as he could. So it was not long before he was back at work, and he was able to take care of the things he needs to do around their home.

Mary Michelle and her handsome, husband, Tim Partlow, were packing their suitcases last summer, because Mary was going to be part of one of her best friend's wedding, and she had been looking forward to this, ever since her friend, Pam, had invited her to come.

Pam and her fiancée ended up getting married without Mary and Tim there, because Mary suddenly had excruciating pain in her hip, back and legs, and she was in so much pain that it caused her to stay in bed, and she could not sit down without torturing pain. Then Tim and his mother took Mary to doctors, and she did not get any better, also, they went to Mayo Clinic in Rochester, Minnesota, and had different tests done by doctors, and Mary did not get any better.

Of course, I prayed for Mary a lot, but things happen that nobody understands, but Jesus. And Mary Michelle and her husband, Tim, were going to have babies before Christian Michael was born, however, Mary did not carry them to full term because Jesus took them to Heaven where we will all get to see them someday.

Although Christian was healthy, there was a time when his baby brother, Trenton Scott, had a blockage in his intestine that turned into a medical emergency because he was throwing up often, and he was losing weight.

Mary took her little baby, Trenton, who was only a few months old, to the emergency room in a hospital close to their home. The doctors ended up sending Trenton in a helicopter to a much bigger hospital where he could get better care. Of course, Mary and Tim called as many people as they could to have them pray for their tiny baby, Trenton, and God miraculously healed him, and Trenton did not have to undergo painful surgery. Then after a few days in the hospital, Mary and Tim got to take Baby Trenton back home, and he gained weight and started trying to talk as much as he could. Thank You, Jesus.

Although I did not get to go and see my baby grandson, Trenton, and his mommy and daddy while Trenton was in the hospital, I cried and prayed to Jesus to please, heal my grandson, Trenton. And give his mommy and daddy the rest and peace that they needed, as Jesus was always with them, and my grandson, Christian Michael.

My youngest daughter, who I call my Little Baby Rachelle, has blessed us so wondrously, because she lives only about twenty-five miles from us now. For she lived clear across the country for several years, and the enemy tried to conquer her health when a painful red place on her lower back swelled up with infection.

Rachelle was working so much that she did not have time to be sick, so when she came home for Thanksgiving that year, the reddened swelled place on her lower back had doubled in size by the time I got her to the doctor. Then the place was lanced and infection came out of it, and packing strips were put into the place on my daughter's lower back where the infection had been removed.

Then Rachelle was tortured again a year and a half later, because another boil came up in the same place where the first one was, which required emergency surgery in the hospital. Then Rachelle was sent home with me from the hospital, and given antibiotics that caused her to feel sick and hurt all over.

I prayed with my Baby Rachelle that God would heal her, and she stayed with me in our home for a few hours, so I could take care of her. Then her boy friend, Josh Sanders, took her home, and her body seemed to heal. And, of course, her boyfriend, Josh, took her to the follow-up doctor appointments, and helped her as much as he could, until, she was well enough to go back to work.

Now, this handsome, young man, Josh Sanders, married my gorgeous Baby Doll Rachelle on May 22, 2010, which was her daddy's birthday, and their wedding was truly, beautiful. Rachelle was by far the most, beautiful angel in the entire universe in her wedding dress that flowed down the aisle of that big church, as she walked toward Josh.

You talk about proud, yes, Josh is a wonderful husband for Mary Rachelle, and Josh's parents and John and I liked each from the first times that we met. Then, before Mary and Josh got married they purchased a beautiful home in Nashville, Tennessee. It only takes a few minutes for us to get together, and spend happy hours talking, working, and eating with each other, because Josh likes to cook out and feed us.

Early one morning, Josh was cooking something on the stove in their new home, and he went out of the room just long enough that the skillet on the stove caught on fire. Then Josh took complete control of getting the fire department called, and got his wife, my Baby Mary Rachelle, and their dog, Juno, and cat, Minou, out of their home, so nobody got hurt. That was a miracle, because the entire home had quickly filled with very, black, thick smoke, which caused Josh and Mary to have a very hard time seeing as they got out of their home. And of course, their cat, Minou, had hidden way upstairs someplace under a bed. Then God helped them get their home fixed up, even nicer, than it was before the fire and smoke damage was done.

Mary and Josh were not married for more than a few months, before Josh had several friends and relatives who died when they were way too young to die. John and I went to one of Josh's brothers, Chris, funeral that was in Tennessee. Of course, it was hard for Mary and Josh because his brother was only a young man when he died, also, it was hard because his brother was a twin, and the family's heart was torn, as they would miss their loved Chris a lot.

However, we will all get to see Chris in Heaven when we get to go through the door that is called "death".

Death is really the door that opens for each and every one of us, when it is our turn to get to be with Jesus in Heaven, and all of our loved ones who have already gone to Heaven.

"Lord Jesus, may Your Light shine upon me and through me, that I may be used of You, Lord, to bless my family. I want to leave yesterdays hurts alone, and live for You, Lord, today and not worry about tomorrow for You are in control of everything, and help me to have love, joy, peace, goodness, gentleness, meekness, self-control, faith, and long suffering so that the Light of Your Glory shines through me, at all times. Lord God, I pray that You, Bless my attitude, so that I may bring glory to Your Name, at all times."

I love you all, my children, and I beg you to, please, live in peace and love one another, as Jesus teaches us to do in "The Holy Bible". And may you, my little children and grandchildren, call one another, and be humble to each other, and give of your own self to each other.

Please, I beg you, my little children and grandchildren, to love one another and live in peace, and do not strife and hold grudges, because you do not want to do anything that will keep you away from each other.

Just think, you will be in Heaven, when you die, and you will have such love, and compassion for one another, that you will think of how much I can help the other person.

Love is nothing, until, it is given away to make somebody else happy. And when you give your love away, do not expect anything in return, because Jesus will give you a blessing that will bring you more joy than you can ever imagine.

Please, I beg you, my little children and grandchildren, love each other, and give of yourself to your sister and brother, mom and dad, children and friends, without consideration to your own feelings that get hurt.

So what if the other person does not give you love, and respect that you do deserve. But you do not have to get it, because God sees all, and God will bless you so very much.

Give yourself up, and call the person that hurts you. And humble yourself before God and that person, no matter how that person treats you in return.

God wants to be the One who blesses you.

Go with the Love and Peace of God, and Do Not Give of Yourself Expecting to Receive Anything from the Other Person. God wants to be the One Who Blesses You My Child. And always know that I am praying for you, my children and my grandchildren.

Have the Love of Jesus Christ, Agape Love, and I will see you in Heaven. But I pray that you do not hurry yourself to die, so you can get to Heaven sooner, because it is a sin to commit suicide.

God has you here for a purpose, and that purpose is for everybody to serve, and praise The Lord Jesus Christ, and let your light so shine that the world sees Christ in you.

I will not die, until Jesus is ready to take me to Heaven. You do not try to do anything that might enable you to die, before Jesus is ready for you to die.

Just because somebody dies, that does not mean that Jesus Christ is through using them on this earth. Sometimes, bad things happen to good people, and they die before their time.

However, the people who die before their time, who are forgiven children of God, who have their sins taken away, and Jesus living in their hearts, go to Heaven when they die. I know we do miss them, and that causes sadness and loneliness for us.

But just think about it, that when anybody dies who has asked Jesus to take their sins away, and come into their heart and life, they go to Heaven, and they are with Jesus. Yes! Thank You, Lord Jesus. Oh, how I love You, Jesus!

Scripture quotations are taken from The New King James version of <u>The Holy Bible</u>.

Additional quotations are noted within the text, and some of my beliefs are taken from The Missionettes Handbook affiliated with the Assemblies of God.

Dedication

<><><><><><><><><><><><><><><><><><><><><><><><><><><><>

To all of my friends and family, and most of all to my husband, John, for helping me to have the strength and courage to work through hurtful memories that were conquering me for most of my life, I want to thank you.

Picture by permission of Hoyt Wedding Photography, Catlin, IL
Daughter Michelle and flower girl Brittany at my wedding

Picture by permission of Hoyt Wedding Photography, Catlin, IL
Daughter Rachelle and ring bearer Jason at my wedding

Picture by permission of Hoyt Wedding Photography, Catlin, IL

Mom and my brother Jim at my wedding

Picture by permission of Hoyt Wedding Photography, Catlin, IL

Mother-in-law and nephew Drew at my wedding

Picture by permission of Hoyt Wedding Photography, Catlin, IL
My son Mike

Picture by permission of Hoyt Wedding Photography, Catlin, IL
Mr. and Mrs. John Reed

Picture by permission of Hoyt Wedding Photography, Catlin, IL
Wedding Party

Picture by permission of Hoyt Wedding Photography, Catlin, IL
Wedding Reception

My mother-in-law, Irene Reed, and sister-in-law,
Linda Kelley, with me at Mike and Stacy's wedding

Wedding of Stacy Jo Wininger and Mike Proctor

Me with my grandchildren Samuel, Elijah, Hannah, & son Mike

Wedding of Cindy Humphrey and Grant Reed

Mr. and Mrs. Grant Reed

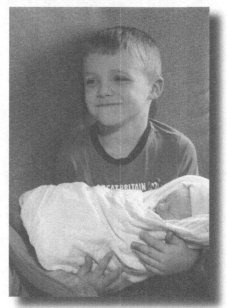

Grandsons Isaac and Caleb Reed

Wedding of Mary Michelle Partlow and Timothy Partlow

Mr. and Mrs. Timothy Partlow

My grandsons Christian and Trenton Partlow
with their parents

Wedding of Mary Rachelle Proctor and Josh Sanders

Mr. and Mrs. Josh Sanders

About the Author

◇◇

Mary Proctor Reed BSRN began life as a Pentecostal minister's daughter, and subsequently married a Pentecostal preacher, who died from melanoma cancer. In order to support her family, she entered nursing school, and earned her BSRN degree, and after gaining experience in several hospital environments, she developed her own private successful business caring for terminally ill patients, resulting in meeting her current husband who was an executive in a major corporation. Her interests have always been in studying God's Word, and being involved in personal ministries, and, today, she continues caring for others, writing and fishing.

NOTES

NOTES